Wood Stoves

Wood Stoves

How to Make and Use Them

Ole Wik

Photographs by Manya Wik

ALASKA NORTHWEST PUBLISHING COMPANY
Anchorage, Alaska

Second printing 1978

Library of Congress cataloging in publication data:
Wik, Ole, 1939-
    Wood stoves.
    Bibliography: p.
    1.   Stoves, Wood.   I.   Wik, Manya.   II.   Title.
TH7438.W55   697'.22   77-21710
ISBN 0-88240-083-5

Grateful acknowledgment is given to the following companies for
permission to reproduce photographs and drawings: Ashley-Spark
Distributors, Inc. Atlanta Stove Works, Inc. Autocrat Corporation.
Blazing Showers. Colorado Tent & Awning Co. Empire-Detroit Steel
Division, Detroit Steel Corporation. Fatsco Stoves. Fire-View®
Distributors. L.W. Gay Stove Works, Inc. Greenbriar Products Inc.
Jøtul, Inc. Kickapoo Stove Works, Ltd. King Products Division, Martin
Industries. Kristia Associates. Locke Stove Co. Louisville Tin & Stove
Co. Malleable Iron Range Co. Markade-Winnwood. Merry Music Box.
Patented Manufacturing Co. Portland Stove Foundry, Inc. Riteway
Manufacturing Co. Shipmate Stove Division, Richmond Ring Co.
Southport Stoves. Torrid Manufacturing Co., Inc. Union Stove Works,
Inc. United States Stove Co. Vermont Woodstove Co. Washington
Stove Works.

Design and illustrations by Jon. Hersh

Alaska Northwest Publishing Company
Box 4-EEE, Anchorage, Alaska 99509
Printed in U.S.A.

For Alexander John Klistoff Sr.,
Master Welder

Contents

PART ONE—USING WOOD STOVES

Chapter 1. Why Wood?   1
How I got started with wood stoves. Some comments on energy,
economics and ecology.

Chapter 2. About Wood Stoves   4
Common elements. Increasing specialization. Diversity of types.
Wood range. Wood cookstove. Combination range. Kitchen
heater. Franklin stove. Freestanding fireplace-stove.
Pot-bellied stove. Parlor stove. Box stoves (cast iron; sheet steel).
Airtight heater. Cabinet heater. Downdraft stove. Wood furnace.
Standing heater. Collapsible stove. Laundry heater. Galley
range. Marine fireplace. Marine cabin heater. Caboose stove.
Wood-fired water heater. Drum heater. Barrel stove kit.

Chapter 3. About Ovens   20
Integral ovens. Stovepipe ovens. Stove-top ovens.

Chapter 4. About Stovepipes   22
Function. Sizes, types, finishes. Joints. Adapters. Elbows.
Dampers. Tees, draft correctors. Stack robbers.

Chapter 5. Stove Accessories   29
Poker. Ash hoe. Shovel. Whisk broom. Tongs. Gloves. Trivet.
Foil door closure pad. Cleaning tools. Wire brush. Stove polish.
Stove pad. Ash can.

Chapter 6. About Wood   32
All wood is not created equal. Different types: dry, half-dry,
punky, pitchy, green, driftwood. Different species.

Chapter 7. Using Wood Stoves   37
Fire as a living thing. Starting a fire. Getting a stove to draw.
Rekindling a small fire. Heating: life cycle of a fire. Moderating a
fire. Taming a stove that won't shut down. Holding a fire
overnight. Keeping a small fire. Incinerating. Ashes.

Chapter 8. Cooking With Wood Stoves   53
Frying. Roasting. Simmering. Pressure cooking. Toasting.
Charcoal cooking. Baking with and without an oven.

Chapter 9. Stove Safety   61
Suggestions for safe location, installation, use and maintenance. The creosote problem. Stack fires. Soot removers. More safety suggestions.

Chapter 10. Getting Wood   69
Where. Types of saws. Sharpening saws. Sawbucks. Splitting wood. Wood carrier.

Chapter 11. The Personality of Wood Stoves   80
Stove idiosyncrasies. Stove talk. Reading smoke signals from the stovepipe.

PART TWO — MAKING WOOD STOVES

Chapter 12. Techniques Versus Attitudes   84
You can do more than you may think.

Chapter 13. How to Build the Three-Way Oil-Barrel Stove   86
Step-by-step instructions on how to build a stove out of a single oil drum.

Chapter 14. About Efficiency   106
A complicated concept. Definition: Efficiency of combustion, efficiency of heat transfer, overall efficiency. Experiments on relative and absolute efficiency.

Chapter 15. Elements of Design   111
The design process. Function. Placement. Shape. Materials. Size. Seams. Doors. Hinges. Latches. Stovepipe collars. Baffles. Ovens. Smoke by-passes. Cleanouts. Draft systems: controls; primary and secondary drafts. Hot-air systems. Hot-water systems. Shelves. Legs. Firebrick. Grates. Ash pans and ash doors. Fastenings. Budget. Flow chart.

Chapter 16. Oil-Barrel Stoves   134
Types of drums. How to reseal a drum after installing a baffle. Whole-barrel stoves (horizontal; vertical). Two-thirds-barrel stoves (vertical; vertical with oven; horizontal round; horizontal squared). One-third-barrel stoves (square; round; oval). Half-cylinder stoves. Half-cylinder with cast-iron stove top. Welded stoves of oil-barrel steel.

Chapter 17. Sheet-Metal Stoves   149
Stovepipe-steel stove. Sheet-steel stove with cast-iron top. The
Ideal Stove. The Super Yukon. The Larry Gay Stove. The Dual-
Fire Range.

Chapter 18. Tin-Can Stoves and Emergency Stoves   155
Five-gallon-can stoves (round and square; horizontal and
vertical). Twenty-five-gallon-can camp stove. Nesting stovepipes.
Tin-can pipeless stove. Tin-can stove with tin-can pipe.
Outboard-tank stove.

Chapter 19. Coking Stoves   162
Definition. Principle of operation. The draft problem. Ted
Ledger's Two-Barrel Stove. Ted Ledger's Coking Stove.
Hypothetical coking stove design. The rotary grate. Stove with
separate coking compartment.

Chapter 20. Stove-Top and Stovepipe Ovens   168
Stove-top single can. Double can, insulated. Stovepipe oven
principle of operation. Tin can and sheet steel. Round, square,
octagonal. Cleaning device.

Chapter 21. Making Stovepipe, Dampers and Adapters   173
Making stovepipe. How to form crimping. How to make dampers
(flat; curved; sleeve). How to make dripless adapters. Tin-can
adapters.

Chapter 22. Hot-Water Systems   181
Stove-top can. How to mend a leaky hot-water can. Built-in
reservoir. Firebox coils. Self-circulating baseboard heater.
Stovepipe or chimney coils. Chip heater. Oil-barrel laundry
heater.

Chapter 23. Epilogue   188
An invitation for feedback.

Appendix: List of Manufacturers   189
Manufacturers of wood stoves and related equipment.

Bibliography   194

Acknowledgments

Many of my friends will recognize their stoves and their ideas in these pages. This is especially true of Oliver Cameron, who helped me get started on my very first homemade stove, and whose creations are sprinkled throughout this book. For favors large and small, I would also like to thank Scotty Bacon, Don Bucknell, Truman Cleveland, Dan Denslow, Tommy Douglas, Nelson Griest, Larry Gay, Jack Hebert, Keith Jones, Mike Jones, Howard and Seth Kantner, Ted Ledger, Pete MacManus, George Melton, Pat Reinhard, Mike Schieber, Bob Schiro and Don Williams.

I am also grateful to my wife, Manya, for much helpful feedback on the manuscript; to her dad, A. J. Klistoff Sr., for translating my stove designs into beautifully welded steel; to the staffs of the Alternative Sources of Energy Lending Library and the Seattle Public Library for help in obtaining various research materials; and to Dave and Kaye Rue and Barbara Donnelly for letting me use the schoolhouse when the cabin was too hectic for writing.

Finally I would like to offer thanks to the craftsmen from all over Alaska whose designs appear in these pages, and who are carrying on the art of building wood stoves by hand.

Part One
Using Wood Stoves

Chapter 1
Why Wood?

When I first went to live in the Far North, I knew next to nothing about wood stoves. But I was firmly committed to wood heat, so I looked through the mail-order catalogs, picked out a model that looked promising, and sent off the order. Freezeup was well under way by the time my cabin was built, and still there was no word on the stove. I wrote to the supplier, who replied that he was out of stoves and had put my money on account.

So there I was, 35 miles above the Arctic Circle, 3 miles from a small Eskimo village served only twice a week by mail plane (weather permitting), 250 miles from Fairbanks and the nearest source of commercial wood stoves. It would take weeks for a stove to arrive through the mail, and the temperature was already getting down to -10°F at night. I would soon have to return the little Yukon stove I had borrowed.

If I were to have a stove, I would clearly have to build it myself. So I went to the village, bought a leaker oil drum for $1, and arranged for a friend to bring it to my camp with his dog team. I cut up the drum with the few simple tools that were at hand, and started bolting the parts together. I made a few blunders as I went along, and got more and more discouraged about the probable outcome. But there was no choice; I had to keep going.

Finally the stove was finished. I attached an elbow and two joints of stovepipe, loaded the firebox with wood, pulled a bit of loose birch bark from a tree for kindling, and lit it up. I really didn't expect much. But when the wood caught fire, the stove started drawing and puffing like a little locomotive, and soon I could see the paint on the barrel metal begin to blister and peel from the heat. Now I began to get excited; this thing was going to work! I went into the cabin for the kettle and soon boiled up a congratulatory cup of tea.

From that day on, I have been fascinated with designing, making and using wood stoves. That first little stove served all of my heating and cooking needs for two full winters, and then did service as a tent stove and laundry-water heater as I moved on to other designs. Progress continues, but it is time now to share what I have learned, and to get in touch with others around the country who are engaged in similar studies and perhaps exchange ideas.

Figure 1.1—My first stove.

Wood has been man's primary fuel for most of his existence, and in many parts of the world it is still the dominant fuel. When I first came North in 1964, only a few households in the nearby Eskimo village could afford to use the only alternative fuel, stove oil. But with the wave of relative prosperity that began to sweep over the valley in the late 1960's, more and more families switched to the prestigious new fuel, and today only 5 households out of 29 rely solely on firewood for space heating.

So here we have a small community, surrounded by tundra and forest, switching from an inexhaustible supply of free firewood to a diminishing supply of increasingly expensive oil. The village mirrors the nation; Americans are surrounded by unused energy sources, yet they become increasingly dependent on distant sources of heating fuels.

The big fuel scares of recent years have generated wide debate over the American energy appetite. Shouldn't we move toward renewable sources of energy whenever possible? Shouldn't we cut back drastically on energy use? Shouldn't we use the complex organic molecules found in petroleum for making pharmaceuticals, polymers and special lubricants rather than burning them for their simple heat content? Can we long afford the environmental and economic burdens of dependence on fuels that are increasingly distant, scarce and costly?

Wood stoves are not the whole answer to the American fuel problem, but at the household level they can make a major contribution to energy self-sufficiency. There is evidence that more and more people are turning in this direction. Permits for gathering firewood on public lands are up sharply, and some wood-stove price lists indicate that certain models must be ordered as much as 24 months in advance.

In this rush to wood stoves, it is altogether likely that many people will pick the wrong stoves for their needs. Others may get stoves that are reasonably well suited to their situations, but may not know how to get the most out of them. You should find solutions to both problems here.

I hope that those readers who are toying with the idea of building a stove will find ideas and encouragement in these pages, and go ahead with their projects. I hope that those who have already built homemade stoves will share their successes (and failures) with me, so that I may pass them on to others.

Figure 1.2—Toward ecologically sound heating: Dead wood cut by hand and hauled with the aid of one dog. The wood ash should be returned to the forest to complete the cycle.

Chapter 2
About Wood Stoves

The first colonists to reach the American shores relied on local rocks and mud to construct their heating sytems. Whether by necessity or custom, these open fireplaces retained a dominant place in homes even as the emergent cities grew large enough to threaten local firewood supplies. But by that time, foundries had begun turning out cast-iron stoves which were more efficient than fireplaces and which gradually took their place as a heat source. The process of evolution has now generated a remarkable variety of wood stoves.

All modern wood stoves retain certain features of their most remote ancestors: a firebox to hold the burning wood, a draft

Figure 2.1—Cookstoves are generally poor for serious heating, and heaters are usually unhandy for cooking. Some people get around the problem by installing two stoves. Here a wood-burning range has been teamed up with a wood-burning airtight heater.

opening to admit air to the fire, a flue to permit smoke to escape. However, increasing specialization in function has led to striking differences in how these common elements are combined.

There are some truly excellent wood heaters on the market today, and some remarkable cookstoves; but the cookstoves are generally poor for serious heating, and the heaters are usually quite unhandy for cooking. The reason lies in basic structural differences between the two types. A good cookstove requires a small firebox to contain an intense fire right up underneath the cooking surface, and insulated sides to prevent excessive heat loss to the kitchen. A good wood heater, by contrast, needs a large firebox to hold a long-lasting fire, and large, bare sides to encourage maximum heat transfer to the room.

As wood-stove specialization continues, it becomes easier to buy the right stove for one's needs. By the same token, it is easier to buy the wrong kind. Let's survey the various types of stoves that are commercially available in the United States today, and see what the market offers. (For a list of manufacturers, see the Appendix. Homemade stoves are covered in Part II.)

WOOD RANGE (Figure 2.2). This is Grandma's classic kitchen stove. The product of generations of use and development, it is unexcelled for cooking and baking. The stove top is generally made

Figure 2.2—Model 51 15 LB wood range by Atlanta Stove Works. The firebox is at the left, the oven in the middle, and a hot-water reservoir at the right, with a faucet behind the door.

of warp-proof cast iron, in several sections. The section over the firebox usually has one or more circular openings for adding wood or for stirring the fire with the poker. The body of the stove is made of sheet steel and the sides are insulated. Various accessories are available, including hot-water reservoirs, warming shelves and towel-drying racks.

WOOD COOKSTOVE (Figure 2.3). This is essentially a stripped-down, simplified, miniaturized version of a wood range.

COMBINATION RANGE (Figure 2.4). Combination cookstoves provide a sort of halfway house for those who would

5

Figure 2.3 (*left*)—Model 8316 Winner cast-iron cookstove by Atlanta Stove Works. The firebox is at upper left, the oven at lower right.

Figure 2.4 (*right*)—Model CE119Y Monarch "Duo-Oven" combination electric coal/wood range by Malleable Iron Range Company. The firebox is at the left, four electric burners at the right. The oven can be heated by either wood or electricity. If the wood fire dies down, the electric oven unit will automatically maintain the temperature set on the dial.

like to switch over to wood without entirely giving up the advantages of their electric or gas ranges. These stoves are fully capable of cooking and baking with wood alone, but they are also fitted with conventional burners. Thus, instant spot heat is always available for rush meals, for summer afternoons too hot for wood-stove cookery, and for times when the woodbox happens to be empty. The ovens are fitted with thermostats, which afford a convenience Grandma never dreamed of: If the wood fire should dwindle, the conventional energy source takes over and maintains the oven at the desired temperature.

KITCHEN HEATER (Figure 2.5). This is essentially a wood range with the oven cut off. Simply styled in white enamel, a kitchen heater can be placed next to a conventional gas or electric stove to provide a bit of extra heat to the home, or to keep the stew pot gently simmering all day long.

FRANKLIN STOVE (Figure 2.6). The classic Franklin stove represents a first step in overcoming the notorious inefficiency of a fireplace without completely sacrificing the undeniable appeal of an open fire. The Franklin features folding doors that can be left open (to give a view of the burning logs) or closed (to convert the unit into a stove). Although advances in technology and design have produced more efficient stoves, the old-style Franklin retains a considerable following, and foundries still turn them out.

6

Figure 2.5 (*left*)Model 24PY Monarch kitchen heater by Malleable Iron Range Company.
Figure 2.6 (*right*)—Model 261 Franklin fireplace heater with optional barbecue grill by United States Stove Company.

FREESTANDING FIREPLACE-STOVE. The concept of a combination fireplace and stove has been carried forward to the point that the results can no longer be termed Franklins. One line of descent leads to the Fire-View (Figure 2.7), a radiant heater fitted with a removable tempered-glass window for viewing the burning

Figure 2.7—Wood heater by Fire-View Distributors. Inner collapsible steel door is open, so that the fire is visible through the tempered-glass window, which may also be removed when an open fire is desired. The steel door allows you to close down the heater to maintain a fire through the night.

logs. Another leads to beautifully styled cast-iron units with tightly fitting, swing-away doors, such as the Jøtul No. 4 (Figure 2.8), or the Morsø No. 1125. And yet another leads to fireplaces that are completely freestanding, such as the Washington Stove Works' Zodiac (Figure 2.9).

The Greenbriar fireplace-stove (Figure 2.10) features an optional hot-water coil which captures heat from stack gases just as they are about to pass into the chimney. The hot water can be circulated to existing baseboard radiators, to hot-water heating

Figure 2.8 (*left*)—Combi-Fire No. 4 by Jøtul. A heavy cast-iron door converts the unit into a heater when it is closed, and swings away beneath the firebox when an open fire is desired. The door handle is visible at the bottom of the stove. Figure 2.9 (*right*)—The Zodiac freestanding fireplace by Washington Stove Works.

Figure 2.10—The Greenbriar fireplace by Greenbriar Products, with optional Pyrex glass door in place. An optional water coil just beneath the flue captures waste heat; the hot water can be piped to conventional heating systems or to storage tanks of solar heating systems.

systems, or to heat exchangers placed in the ductwork of forced-air heating systems, greatly increasing the overall efficiency of the unit. In a truly energy-efficient house, the hot water can also be piped to the storage tank of the solar heating system.

POT-BELLIED STOVE (Figure 2.11). The pot-bellied stove dates from the days when cast iron was the most easily available type of metal for stove construction. Like the Franklin, it has built-in nostalgia. Rugged and durable, it burns coal, wood or a combination of both.

Figure 2.11 (*left*)—Model 13, the Cannonball pot-bellied stove by Washington Stove Works.
Figure 2.12 (*right*)—Model V parlor stove by Washington Stove Works.

PARLOR STOVE (Figure 2.12). In the days before central heating, parlor stoves were used in those rooms where appearance was a consideration. They are large cast-iron heaters decorated with greater or lesser amounts of nickel trim "gingerbread."

BOX STOVE I: CAST IRON (Figure 2.13). Box stoves also trace their origin to the days before the invention of rolling mills and sheet steel. Any foundry could easily produce the various plates

Figure 2.13—No. 38 Monitor cast-iron box stove by the Portland Stove Foundry Company.

that lock together to form the stove's basic box shape. The result is a stove that is simple and durable, with a flat top that is handy for certain kinds of cooking. Unfortunately, the older models are rather inefficient; since they have no baffles, the hot gases are free to

9

escape directly up the stovepipe. Air leakage between the plates is also a problem, making it more or less difficult to control the fire.

European designers have produced some striking cast-iron box stoves that offer markedly improved performance, along with a more refined appearance (Figure 2.14). They feature slanting baffles or top-mounted gallery boxes that force the smoke to take a longer path before reaching the flue, giving up heat along the way. They also have improved seams which permit very little air to reach

Figure 2.14 (*left*)—Morsø Model 2B0 with heat exchanger, from Denmark. Distributed in the U.S. by Southport Stoves.

Figure 2.15 (*below*)—Cross-section of the Morsø Model 2B0. Due to the baffle in the upper part of the firebox, the logs burn from front to back, like a cigar. Even without the heat exchanger, the hot gases have to take a long path to reach the flue, giving up heat along the way. The heat exchanger draws out still more heat that would otherwise escape up the stovepipe.

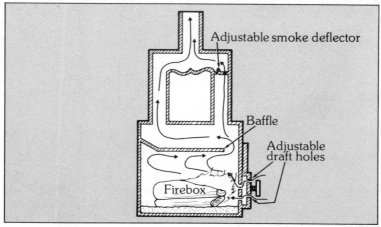

Adjustable smoke deflector

Baffle

Adjustable draft holes

Firebox

the fire. As a result, the stoves deliver far more heat per cord of wood burned than a stove without baffles, and do a much better job of holding a fire overnight (Figure 2.15).

BOX STOVE II: SHEET STEEL. The invention of sheet steel and the means for welding it together led to great advances in wood-stove technology. For the first time, it was possible to design a stove with truly airtight seams, and so to gain almost complete control over the rate of combustion. Use of sheet steel also freed stove designers to think in terms of innovative shapes, such as the Bader Burn Right (Figure 2.16), and portability, exemplified by the Yukon and sheep herder stoves (Figures 2.17 and 2.18).

Figure 2.16 (*left*)—The Bader Burn Right by Kickapoo Stove Works, Ltd. Figure 2.17 (*below left*)—A lightweight Yukon stove carried by a passing musher. The stovepipe is tapered, and nests inside the firebox; when installed, the bottom of the pipe forms the rear leg of the unit. Figure 2.18 (*below right*)—Sheep herder stove with built-in oven, formerly distributed by Colorado Tent & Awning Company, but currently unavailable commercially.

AIRTIGHT HEATER (Figure 2.19). If sheet steel is made thin enough, seams can be made by rolling rather than welding. Airtight heaters carry lightness to the extreme; the small and medium-sized models can even be sent through the mails. (Large models, still within weight limits, run afoul of size restrictions.) Since they use a

11

minimum amount of materials and are easily fabricated, airtights are inexpensive. They are not at all fussy about the type of wood they use and are easy to regulate, so it is easy to maintain an overnight fire.

Figure 2.19—Reeves airtight heater by Empire-Detroit Steel Division, Detroit Steel Corporation.

The thin walls of an airtight heater naturally burn out more quickly than those of heavier, more expensive stoves, but the useful life can be extended by protecting the stove from moisture when not in use and by selecting a size large enough that it can loaf most of the time.

CABINET HEATER (Figure 2.20). This type of stove consists of a heavy, airtight steel firebox encased in an attractive enameled cabinet. The firebox, which is designed to take large sticks of wood, is fitted with a heavy, gasketed cast-iron door that closes tightly. Incoming air is preheated and distributed along the bed of coals, so that the wood burns out evenly. Ashes fall through the grate into an ash pan that can be emptied without undue mess. Most models

Figure 2.20—End view of Autocrat Model 6724 cabinet heater, showing large feed-door opening, cast sectional linings, ribbed cast-iron grate, cast-iron flue collar, ash door and ash pan.

have provision for an optional fan that blows heated air out at floor level, helping to smooth out the temperature gradient that tends to form between the floor and the ceiling in rooms heated by wood stoves.

Cabinet heaters incorporate another giant step in wood-stove effectiveness: the automatic, thermostatically controlled draft. A bimetallic spring—reacting to the temperature of the stove—automatically opens or closes the draft to maintain the desired heat output.

Some cabinet heaters are characterized by especially fine engineering and attention to detail. One of the more innovative designs was created by the Riteway Company in an effort to achieve the elusive goal of complete combustion of smoke, thus increasing the total heat output and minimizing soot build-up in the chimney. In the Riteway 2000 (Figure 2.21), the smoke is forced to pass near the zone of primary combustion before entering a special combustion flue. A stream of "secondary" air mixes with the heated gases within this flue, encouraging final combustion.

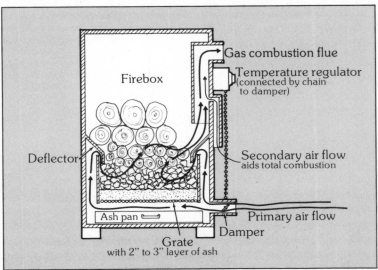

Figure 2.21—Cross-section of the Riteway 2000 radiant heater by the Riteway Manufacturing Company.

DOWNDRAFT STOVE. A downdraft stove may be defined as one in which the smoke must pass *through* the bed of coals before reaching the flue. In so doing, the smoke is exposed to extremely high temperatures and is consumed. I know of only one wood stove on the market today that meets this definition: the DownDrafter, manufactured by the Vermont Woodstove Company.

In the DownDrafter (Figures 2.22 and 2.23), slanting grates funnel the hottest coals toward the choke points through which exhaust gases must exit. Complete combustion is indicated by a clean, bluish flame, actually visible through special viewing ports. To increase heat-transfer efficiency, the DownDrafter incorporates an isolated inner chamber through which room air is circulated by a blower. A special thermostatic control system—reacting to *stack*

Figure 2.22 (*left*)—The DownDrafter (patent applied for) by Vermont Woodstove Company.

Figure 2.23 (*below*)—Cross-section of the DownDrafter. Wood is gradually converted to charcoal as volatile substances are driven off by the heat. Slanting grates funnel the hottest coals to two choke points. Smoke must pass through the coals in order to gain access to the stovepipe, and is heated and completely burned in the process.

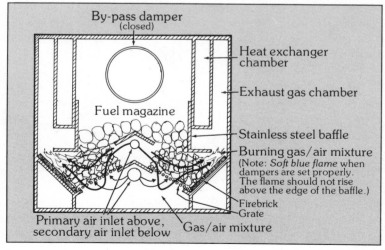

By-pass damper
(closed)

Heat exchanger chamber

Exhaust gas chamber

Fuel magazine

Stainless steel baffle

Burning gas/air mixture
(Note: *Soft blue flame* when dampers are set properly. The flame should not rise above the edge of the baffle.)

Firebrick
Grate

Primary air inlet above, secondary air inlet below

Gas/air mixture

temperature—regulates both the blower and the air supplied to the fire through the drafts. The blower operates only when excess heat is available. (Continuous operation could result in overcooling the stack gases, leading to reduced draft and an increased tendency for deposits to form in the chimney.)

Note that a downdraft stove might also be called a "coking" stove. The volatile substances are driven out of the fresh wood at the top of the firebox and pass down through the coals, where they burn completely, to provide the heat needed to continue the wood-distillation process. By the time the wood has been completely stripped of volatiles and has become charcoal, it has settled down into the zone of primary combustion to provide the fuel for coking the next charge of wood.

WOOD FURNACE (Figure 2.24). Like other units designed for heavy-duty heating of large spaces, wood furnaces make no attempt at beauty; they just sit in the cellar and work. They take large logs, so they do not have to be tended more than a couple of times a day, and they hold a fire all night, or longer, on a single

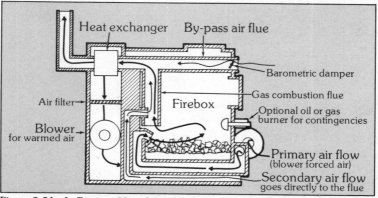

Figure 2.24—In Riteway Manufacturing Company's wood furnace, a forced draft is created in the firebox by a thermostatically controlled blower. Secondary air passes into the gas combustion flue inside the firebox. A barometric damper permits room air to flow into the by-pass air flue, where it mixes with flue gases and helps prevent creosote deposits. Return air is preheated at the heat exchanger, blown over the furnace body and heated further, then passes through the duct system of the house.

charge. They can be connected to the house's ductwork to provide forced-air heat, and some models are even designed to operate by gravity flow in the event the blowers are knocked out by a power failure.

A wood furnace can be mounted beside a conventional furnace, which automatically takes over if the wood alone can't supply enough heat. Alternatively, dual-fuel units are available; they burn both wood and oil or natural gas in the same firebox. When a charge of wood burns out, oil or gas kicks in so that a steady temperature is maintained in the house.

STANDING HEATER (Figure 2.25). At least two European firms—Styria of Austria and Jøtul of Norway—produce a kind of space heater not manufactured in the United States. These heaters feature a firebox at the bottom, with loading and secondary-draft doors higher up. Some models burn coal, coke and peat as well as wood.

COLLAPSIBLE STOVE (Figure 2.26). Lightweight, knockdown stoves are suitable for camp use or for emergency backup heating systems. The Dynapac Stovaway, for example, is

Figure 2.25 (*left*)—Standing heater by Styria of Austria, distributed by Merry Music Box.
Figure 2.26 (*below*)—The Camper's Companion collapsible stove by Washington Stove Works.

packed in a box measuring only 21 by 26 by 27 inches, and can easily be stored in a closet. If provision were made beforehand for fuel and for venting the smoke through an existing flue, fireplace or window, such a stove would be cheap insurance against a natural disaster, power blackout or fuel shortage. If such a reserve stove kept the house's plumbing from freezing only once, it would pay for itself many times over.

LAUNDRY HEATER (Figure 2.27). This is a small cast-iron stove with an oversized top designed to accommodate a large laundry tub. In the old days these stoves were also used for heating garment-pressing irons.

GALLEY RANGE (Figure 2.28). Wood ranges for shipboard use are equipped with removable rails and rolling bars to keep pots from shifting around or falling off the stove when the vessel rocks in the waves. In other respects they are much like conventional wood ranges, except that they are available in remarkably small sizes.

MARINE FIREPLACE (Figure 2.29). The Richmond Ring Company offers an open-fireplace heater that combines the cheeriness of an open fire with the extreme compactness required for shipboard use. With the cast-bronze kindler door closed, the unit becomes a circulating heater; room air enters the cavity walls at the bottom, is warmed, and flows by convection out of ports on top of the cabinet.

Figure 2.27 (*left*)—Model 488 Sun laundry heater formerly manufactured by King Products Division, Martin Industries, but now discontinued. Other models are available.

Figure 2.28 (*right*)—The Neptune galley range by Washington Stove Works.

Figure 2.29 (*left*)—Model 201CH Shipmate open-fireplace cabin heater by Richmond Ring Company.

Figure 2.30 (*right*)—Skippy cabin heater by Richmond Ring Company.

MARINE CABIN HEATER (Figure 2.30). These midget stoves are handy for heating small areas, such as the cabin on a boat. Like marine ranges, they have toprails to keep pots from falling in rough weather. The little units have so much charm that many are undoubtedly purchased for use ashore.

CABOOSE STOVE (Figure 2.31). This is another small unit designed to burn coal, briquets or short sticks of wood.

WOOD-FIRED WATER HEATER. As far as I know, no United States manufacturer currently offers a water heater fueled by wood, but Modern Kit Sales has announced plans to introduce one.

DRUM HEATER (Figure 2.32). This is a cylindrical sheet-steel drum lined with firebrick and fitted with cast-iron legs, feed door and stovepipe collar.

Figure 2.31 (*left*)—Low caboose stove No. 249 by Union Stove Works.
Figure 2.32 (*right*)—Warm-Ever drum heater by Locke Stove Company. This is available in two lengths: 21¼ and 30¾ inches, substantially smaller than a conventional oil-barrel stove. Eight sections of firebrick for lining are included with the smaller model, twelve with the larger.

BARREL STOVE KIT (Figure 2.33). Several companies offer cast-iron or welded-steel fittings for converting an ordinary 30- or 55-gallon oil barrel or a 100-pound grease pail into a heater. These kits bridge the gap between commercial units and homemade stoves, which will be considered in detail in Part Two.

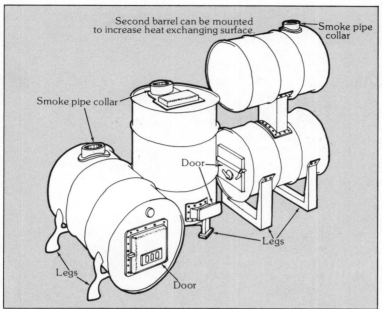

Figure 2.33—Cast-iron fittings for converting an ordinary 55-gallon oil barrel into a wood heater (*left*), by Washington Stove Works. Some companies offer kits for 30-gallon drums and 100-pound grease cans. Kits are also available for converting oil drums into vertical heaters (*middle*), and for mounting one drum atop another as a heat exchanger (*right*). Those shown are welded of 16-gauge steel and are manufactured by Markade-Winnwood.

Chapter 3
About Ovens

Wood-stove ovens fall into three categories: integral ovens, stovepipe ovens and stove-top ovens. Integral ovens are built right into the body of the stove, and generally require a dual smokeway controlled by a sliding baffle or smoke flap. When a fire is being started, the baffle is placed in the open position, allowing smoke and hot gases to pass directly out the flue. Once the fire is going briskly and the draft is well established, the flap can be closed to divert the smoke around and under the oven to heat it.

Kitchen ranges always feature an integral oven, and there are many ways to incorporate one into the design of a homemade stove. In general, it is easiest to maintain a steady baking temperature in a massive stove, but, with practice, one can also turn out excellent baked goods on some very small models.

A stovepipe oven (Figures 3.1 and 3.2) is a double-walled vessel with stovepipe connections at top and bottom. The interior of the oven is heated by smoke passing through the cavity between

Figure 3.1—Stovepipe oven by Louisville Tin & Stove Company.

the walls. Brackets fitted to the inside walls hold shelves for baking pans. Simply by leaving the door ajar, a stovepipe oven can also be used as a "stack robber" to draw extra heat from the flue gases before they escape to the atmosphere.

Stove-top ovens (Figure 3.3) are simply bottomless metal boxes

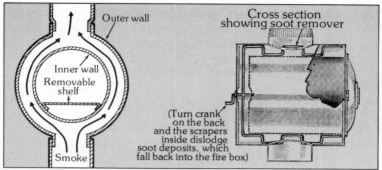

Outer wall

Inner wall
Removable
shelf

Smoke

Cross section
showing soot remover

(Turn crank
on the back
and the scrapers
inside dislodge
soot deposits, which
fall back into the fire box)

Figure 3.2—Stovepipe oven, cross-section.

that sit directly on the stove. Some commercial models have such refinements as insulated cavity walls, hinged doors with see-through glass panels, temperature gauges, and movable wire-grill shelves. Some very serviceable homemade models are nothing more than ordinary 5-gallon cans with one side cut out. Whether

Figure 3.3—A commercial stove-top oven sitting on a homemade oil-barrel stove. On days when a baking fire would overheat the snug cabin, the oven can be used on a gasoline camp stove.

simple or elaborate, stove-top ovens are capable of turning out good breads and pastries on any stove, as long as the stove top can be made hot enough without driving everybody out of the house. In addition, they can be used on gasoline, natural gas, or even electric stoves when it is too hot to fire up the wood stove.

Some tips on baking with integral, stovepipe and stove-top ovens—as well as for baking without an oven—are provided in Chapter 8.

21

Chapter 4
About Stovepipes

The most obvious function of the stovepipe is to carry smoke, water vapor and fine ash from the firebox to the atmosphere. But another function, equally important, is to create the draft, or suction, needed to keep air flowing through the firebox.

Many times I've set up our little laundry stove outdoors in the summertime, when it is too hot to have a fire in the cabin. It might seem that a stovepipe would be unnecessary out there in the open air, but without pipe, the smoke can't tell the difference between the stoke hole and the stovepipe port, and the fire burns sluggishly. As soon as a couple of sections of stovepipe are attached, however, the smoke moves up the pipe and fresh air moves into the firebox to take its place. The oxygen perks up the fire, the stovepipe heats up and draws still better, and the combustion cycle goes on and on.

A stovepipe acts like a siphon, but in reverse; it moves smoke from a lower to a higher level. Like a siphon, its effectiveness is proportional to the difference in elevation between the two ends. In practical terms, this means that a stovepipe can be made to draw more strongly by simply adding another section.

Most commercial wood stoves take pipe 5, 6 or 7 inches in diameter, but 4- and 8-inch pipes are also stock items at many hardware stores. Stovepipe is sold open so that it nests for shipment and storage. It has a special self-locking seam that snaps together at the time the pipe is to be installed (Figure 4.1), making a solid, safe unit. Some stoves come with tapered pipe that is designed to nest one section within the next. In some units, the whole set fits right inside the firebox when not in use.

Stovepipe comes in two standard finishes—galvanized and black. Galvanized pipe has a shiny, silvery surface when it is new, but if the pipe is heated past a certain point, the zinc coating alloys with the sheet-steel base and the luster is permanently lost. Black stovepipe has a shiny, blue-black color which also dulls with use; an application of stove polish from time to time will restore the sheen and keep it looking nice.

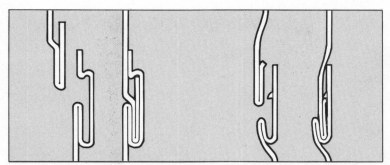

Figure 4.1—Patented self-locking devices on stovepipe by Louisville Tin & Stove Company (*left*) and Ashley-Spark Distributors, Inc. (*right*).

Black stovepipe is less expensive than the galvanized type, but it is also made of a lighter-gauge steel which burns out more quickly. Stovepipes usually burn out first along the seam, and a pipe with reasonably sound walls often has to be discarded just because the seam no longer holds it together properly. I always buy the longer-lasting galvanized pipe. When a section starts to burn out, I replace it immediately rather than risk a house fire. The old pipe may get a few more uses the following summer when we fire up the stove outdoors, but when it becomes unsafe, I junk it without regret.

The standard length of each stovepipe section is 24 inches, but since one end is crimped to fit inside the uncrimped end of the next section, the useful length of each section is 22½ inches. Half-sections are also available.

It may seem logical that the crimped end of a stovepipe ought to be up, so that the smoke has a smooth passage from one pipe section to the next. The problem is that, in cold weather, moisture condenses inside the pipe and then runs back down toward the stove. As soon as the black, watery condensate reaches the first joint, it runs out onto the outer surface of the next section down, creating unsightly streaks which give off an unpleasant odor the next time the stovepipe heats up. After a few weeks the pipes look really bad, and in hard cases, a crust of highly flammable residue may build up where the pipe joins the stove. Thus, an eyesore becomes a safety hazard.

It may seem equally logical that if the crimped ends of the stovepipe sections face down, the edges inside the pipe will catch the smoke and direct it into the room. But it doesn't work that way. Since the draft is a suction phenomenon, air tends to leak *into* the pipe instead. With the crimps down, the condensate funnels right past the junctions, toward the stove, where it eventually evaporates. The outside of the pipe remains spotless (Figure 4.2).

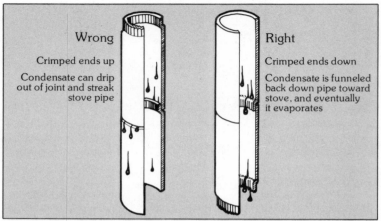

Figure 4.2—Why stovepipe should be installed with the crimped end down.

In warm regions, the stovepipe may never really get cold enough for condensation to occur, but in the North Country it can be a real nuisance. Unfortunately, some stove manufacturers seem to have missed this rather important point. They designed their stovepipe collars so that the pipe has to be connected the messy way, with the crimped ends up. I struggled with this problem for some time before figuring out how to make a simple adapter that eliminates the problem altogether (see Chapter 21). Thompson and Anderson Sheet Metal (Westbrook, Maine 04092) will make adapters to order so that any stove can be used with the stovepipe right side up.

Occasionally, it is necessary to use two different stovepipe diameters in a single installation; for example, when a stove with provision for a 7-inch pipe is used with a 6-inch chimney connection. Several types of reducing and increasing adapters are on the market (Figure 4.3), but again, many are made the wrong way—with the crimped end up. Once more, custom-made adapters are the only answer.

Stoves with the stovepipe collar at the rear require an elbow to make the connection with the vertical stovepipe. A standard one-piece 90-degree elbow is formed from a short piece of pipe by multiple crimps around the circumference, and comes in both light-gauge black and heavy-gauge galvanized finishes.

Figure 4.3—A commercial stovepipe adapter connecting a 6-inch 90-degree elbow to a 5-inch stovepipe. Note that the crimping is toward the top of the adapter. In cold weather, this will lead to stovepipe streaking when sooty condensate drips down the inside of the pipe.

Bends of less than 90 degrees require adjustable elbows. Made up of four swiveling sections, these take any angle from 0 to 90 degrees. Since the seams burn out fairly rapidly and may drip condensate, it is unwise to use this kind of elbow in the full 90 degree position where a solid one-piece model will do.

Most wood-stove setups require a damper in the stovepipe. A damper is merely a slightly undersized, perforated cast-iron disk, mounted on a metal shaft in such a way that it forms a butterfly valve inside the pipe (Figure 4.4). One end of the shaft extends beyond the pipe into the room, and is bent to form a handle. With the damper in the open position, the flue gases have free access to the upper pipe and the atmosphere. With the damper partially or fully closed, gases can escape only through the perforations and the spaces that remain around the edges of the disk.

If two stoves are connected to a single stovepipe, the connection is made by means of a tee. This is merely a short section of standard stovepipe with a collar emerging from it at right angles.

With the addition of a counterbalanced, swiveling flap in the collar opening, a simple tee becomes a draft corrector or draft minder (Figure 4.5). This ingenious device is designed to overcome excessive draft by admitting a regulated amount of air into the stovepipe. This "spoils" the effective draft at the firebox because much of the suction provided by the chimney is pulling air through the tee rather than through the stove.

A draft corrector is set by adjusting the counterbalance weight so that the flap hangs open just enough to correct the draft for calm-weather operation. Then, on windy days, when a gust suddenly increases the suction on the pipe, the flap merely pivots to a more open position, admitting extra air from the room into the stovepipe.

How to Install a Damper

1. Select a damper that matches the stovepipe in size. (It will be somewhat smaller in diameter than the pipe.) Remove the disk from the shaft, noting how the two pieces are held together by the tension of a spring. (Leave the spring on the shaft.)
2. Mark two holes diametrically opposite one another on the stovepipe, about 4 or 5 inches from the upper end.
3. Punch the holes lightly. (A 2x4 or small log makes a handy anvil.)
4. Drill the holes, using a bit somewhat smaller than the diameter of the damper shaft. (If you have no drill, punch through the metal with a nail.)
5. Enlarge the holes one at a time, using the damper shaft as an awl. This will ensure the tight fit necessary to prevent smoke from leaking into the room when the damper is closed.
6. Insert the shaft through one of the holes. Place the disk inside the pipe and thread it onto the shaft. Push the shaft through the bearing holes of the disk and on out the other hole in the pipe. This will require a bit of twisting back and forth.
7. When the shaft is all the way through the pipe and the crank is lined up with the receiver cup in the damper plate, twist until the crank rests in the cup. Release the shaft. The spring will hold everything in place.

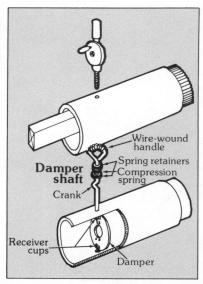

Figure 4.4—Installing a damper.

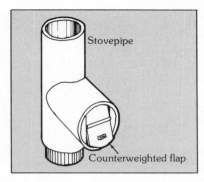

Stovepipe

Counterweighted flap

Figure 4.5 — Barometric draft control, or draft corrector.

The suction on the firebox remains relatively steady, and the fire burns evenly. When the gust subsides, the flap swings right back to the preselected position. The little flap, creaking back and forth all day in response to every gust, keeps you informed on the progress of the storm outside.

Every wood-stove owner eventually wonders how much of the heat in the flue gases could be captured and used to heat the house. Various types of heat exchangers or "stack robbers" have been developed to meet this need. One popular type consists of a series of horizontal tubes in a boxlike container which is mounted between two joints of stovepipe (Figure 4.6). Smoke passing around the tubes heats them, and a small fan blows the hot air out into the room. The energy retrieved from the waste heat far exceeds the energy required to operate the fan, and so the unit pays for itself over a period of time. As an added bonus, the fan helps to break up the hot-air layering that generally occurs in rooms heated by wood stoves.

Figure 4.6 — A commercial stack robber (this one by Torrid Air) can capture significant amounts of heat from flue gases. A fan blows room air through the 10 heat-exchange tubes. The little knob in the center of the array of tubes is the end of the cleaning rod. When it is pulled out, a plate inside slides forward and scrapes accumulated soot from the tubes. The soot then falls back down the stovepipe.

Another simpler type of stack robber consists of a series of shaped metal rings (Figure 4.7) that slip over the first section of stovepipe and act as radiating fins.

Figure 4.7—An inexpensive stovepipe heat-exchange system consisting of slip-on heat fins is produced by **Patented Manufacturing Company.**

This covers the basic stovepipe hardware between the stove and the wall or ceiling. Many kinds of fittings are manufactured for passing stovepipes safely out of a building, and you should discuss them with your local hardware and building-supply dealers.

Chapter 5
Stove Accessories

Day-to-day operation of a wood stove requires a few simple accessories. Each setup has its own particular requirements. This is my personal list:

POKER. This tool is essential for rearranging the wood in the firebox and for raking the coals forward to the draft in those stoves where this is necessary. A poker need not be elaborate; I've gotten by for long periods with nothing more than a green stick. But, naturally, some sort of light metal rod is better. It should have a right-angle crook on the working end.

ASH HOE. A small, fireproof version of the common garden tool, the ash hoe is used to pull ashes forward when emptying the stove or when covering the draft hole in order to seal it when setting an overnight fire. It is also handy for pushing the glowing coals to the back of the stove, as one does when preparing to bake in a stovepipe oven or when setting the fire to hold overnight.

SMALL SHOVEL. This is handy for removing ashes from the firebox, and also for use as a dustpan when the sweepings are to go into the stove. The small models, designed to go with coal scuttles, and the fancier ones, sold as fireplace accessories, both work nicely.

WHISK BROOM. Hung near the stove, a whisk broom makes it easy to sweep up spilled ashes and bits of bark or wood.

TONGS. Either the ordinary kitchen variety or a special cast-iron fireplace pair of tongs is handy for stuffing papers and other refuse into the firebox for disposal, and also for rearranging the wood when the fire is low. I have often used the tongs to place dead charcoal from the previous fire on top of the kindling when I build a new one. Tongs also make it easy to remove tin cans and other metallic debris from the firebox (after incinerating rubbish), even while it is still hot.

GLOVES. I keep a heavy leather gauntlet-type welder's glove near my stove at all times for dealing with an especially hot fire. It is also useful for handling wood that is dripping sticky pitch.

TRIVET. A trivet is an indispensable part of wood-stove cookery. Anything that will keep the cooking pot from direct contact with the hot stove top will do; for example, the lid from a No. 10 can, with tabs bent down around the edges (Figure 5.1).

Figure 5.1—A trivet is an indispensable part of wood-stove cookery. This one was made from oil-barrel metal.

DOOR *PINYA*. A *pinya*—or more stiffly, door closure pad—has a usefulness far exceeding its humble appearance. It consists of a four-ply square of aluminum foil, with or without a very thin layer of fiberglass insulation inside for added bulk. The *pinya* (*pinya* is the local Eskimo all-purpose word corresponding to our "what-cha-ma-call-it"), serves as a cheap, replaceable, custom-made gasket for sealing off the firebox door when setting an overnight fire. Some stoves have doors that don't lend themselves to this sort of gasketing, and others are tight enough that they don't need any help. But many, many stoves can really profit from this simple device; in fact, I learned the trick from a neighbor who invented the first *pinya* to give himself still greater control over his airtight heater.

CLEANING TOOLS. These are necessary for removing soot from most wood stoves. Wood ranges, which have elaborate passageways for conducting the hot gases around and under the oven, are especially likely to collect soot, and are always designed with special cleaning ports to give access to the passages. The standard tool for cleaning out the narrow cavities looks like a thin, double-edged hoe.

Stovepipes also accumulate their share of residue—chiefly carbonaceous deposits derived from unburned volatile substances in the smoke. This crust can be surprisingly thick and tenacious. The only commercial stovepipe-cleaning tool I've seen is a kind of giant bottle brush, made in Austria and sold by Merry Music Box. (For the address, see the listing of manufacturers in the Appendix.) I have always cleaned my own stovepipes with a very simple tool consisting of a folded tin-can lid nailed onto the end of a stick (Figure 5.2).

WIRE BRUSH. Handy for burnishing the stove surfaces and removing caked-on deposits.

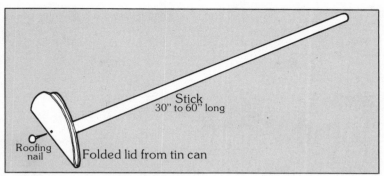

Figure 5.2—Stovepipe cleaning tool.

STOVE POLISH. An application of polish restores a very nice appearance, even on rusty surfaces. Some brands are available in liquid form, but I prefer the kind that comes as a paste in a tube.

STOVE PAD. It is wise to invest in some sort of nonflammable stove pad to protect the floor beneath the stove from radiated heat and from any embers which may fall from the firebox. Commercial pads—consisting of enameled metal over asbestos matting—are available in a variety of sizes. Others can easily be made from sheet metal.

ASH CAN. Some stoves also benefit from a can placed beneath the door to catch falling embers. With some models, sparks will pop right out of the draft opening, so it is well to be sure that either the stove pad or the ash can protects the area where they land.

Stove pads and ash cans bring us into the realm of stove safety, which we'll consider in detail in Chapter 9.

Chapter 6
About Wood

It was my privilege, during my first winter in the Far North, to have access to an entire forest that hadn't been touched for decades. Dry spruce stood everywhere; consequently, that's all I burned. It was only later, after moving to a less favored region, that I was forced by necessity to experiment with other species of trees and with wood in other conditions (such as green, half-dry, punky, pitchy and driftwood). I soon learned that all woods are not created equal, by any means. The same principles apply to the wood types available in other areas, even if the species of trees are different.

Forests in the north are very monotonous compared to those of warmer regions. Our list of firewood species, as a result, is very short: white spruce, black spruce, paper birch, cottonwood, quaking aspen, willow and alder. But since each of these woods may be found in a variety of types (Figure 6.1), we actually do have a fair range of distinct kinds of fuel.

Figure 6.1—Three different grades of white spruce. *Bottom left:* dry wood. Note the cracks. *Bottom right:* half-dry wood, with a darker ring of sapwood just inside the bark. *Top:* punky wood. The spongy texture is very obvious.

The great mainstay of wood-burning stoves throughout most of Alaska is white spruce. (Black spruce is so nearly identical in its firewood properties that, if there is any difference, I have missed it.)

Dry spruce, in the local Eskimo dialect, is called *qirrupiaq*—"real wood." It is easy to light, responds immediately to the draft, gives a hot fire, and leaves a good bed of coals. It is a forgiving wood; even if the fire has been neglected until only a few coals remain, a handful of kindling and a few splits of dry spruce will quickly revive it.

Half-dry spruce comes from trees that are almost, but not quite, dead. When a spruce tree is dying, the layer of sapwood under the bark gets thinner and thinner, the heartwood drier and drier. Once the growing tip of the tree dies, the branches follow, one by one. When only a few branches bear green needles, the tree is prime for cutting (Figure 6.2).

Figure 6.2—A prime half-dry white spruce. Note the dead growing tip and the many dead branches. This tree would yield excellent firewood.

Half-dry spruce combines the advantageous properties of both green and dry wood. If it is laid on a good bed of coals and the draft is opened, it takes right off. If the draft is closed, the wood lies there for a long time, absorbing heat and drying out; the stove marks time while the wood soaks up heat. Thus, half-dry spruce can be used either for instant heat or as a holding wood.

Punky spruce is wood that has begun to decay before the tree dies. Rot begins in the center of the trunk near the bottom, then works its way upward and outward toward the bark. The punky wood is orange-colored with myriad little white spots, like some strange cheese. The fibrous texture is gone, so the wood is very easy to saw but difficult to split evenly.

Occasionally, the core of a spruce is punky, while the outer portion of the trunk is firm and heavily encrusted with pitch (especially around the knots). This pitchy wood is handy for rekindling a small fire, since the pitch melts and runs down onto the coals, where it ignites very easily. Pitchy knots are also handy when baking in a wood range, since they produce a quick, hot flame.

Green spruce has a thick layer of resinous sapwood just beneath the bark, and healthy moist wood from there through the core. It may be burned the same day the tree is cut down, but the considerable energy cost of evaporating the excess moisture will have to be paid by wood already on the fire. It is more efficient to cut and split the wood well ahead of time and let it air-dry for a year—even two—before burning it. Personally, I don't feel right about cutting healthy trees for fuel, and most of the green wood that goes into my stove comes as scrap from building projects. It is handy for holding an overnight fire or for cooling a fire quickly.

Driftwood is always welcome, since the river does the work of hauling it to camp. One spring we made camp along a high riverbank rimmed with a thick deposit of driftwood, and for a month we never had to go more than 20 steps for fuel. Driftwood comes in all types, sizes and conditions, so with a little care in selection, it is possible to find fuel that is suitable for almost any use. Small, dry sticks are fine for cooking, and larger, moister ones are handy for holding a fire. On the minus side, ocean-borne driftwood can carry corrosive salt into the stove, and driftwood from any source is likely to be contaminated with more or less saw-dulling sand and silt. Still, in some circumstances it can be a very satisfactory fuel.

Paper birch is the nearest thing we have to the excellent hardwood fuels of the eastern states. (The rest of our species rank fairly low on any list of preferred woods.) It burns hot, lasts a long time, and produces fine coals. To my mind, the smoke from burning birch is one of the most pleasant smells in the north woods. But in spite of all these fine qualities, I burn very little birch. The living trees are just too beautiful to cut down, and it is hard to find dead ones in burning condition because the bark forms a durable, watertight cylinder that encourages extremely rapid rotting. The odd chunk that comes my way usually goes into the stove at bedtime, when I set the overnight fire.

Cottonwood and aspen rank low on our list of preferred woods. When green they are exceptionally heavy and waterlogged, and when punky they burn without much heat. When properly seasoned they burn well enough, although ash production is high and coal production rather low compared to some other species.

Willows figure prominently in our firewood diet only in spring and summer, when we camp near riverbank thickets. We collect "breakwood," which is anything that can be harvested without an ax or saw (Figure 6.3). Dead willows that are still standing are usually fairly dry, and they make a reasonably good fuel. One man

Figure 6.3—Oliver Cameron ricks up his willows and alders tipi-fashion for drying.

here uses very little else; he makes one trip a day all winter to the thicket across the river, and drags the wood back with one dog and a little sled built around an old pair of skis.

Alders in this area rarely get any thicker than a man's arm, so, as with willows, it takes quite a bit of work to collect any quantity of them. Dry alder can be used much like spruce, although it is a bit slower to start. It produces firm, hot coals, very much like those of birch. Green and half-dry alder is handy for holding fires overnight; it gives a really intense fire when the draft is opened the following morning. Unfortunately, creosote production is high, and this alone is enough to rule out its use in some installations (see Chapter 9 for a discussion of the creosote problem).

Firewood Ratings

COURTESY RITEWAY MANUFACTURING CO.

Wood Variety	Relative Heat	Easy to Burn	Easily Split	Smoke	Sparks
Ash, Red Oak, Beech, White Oak, Birch, Hickory, Hard Maple, Pecan, Dogwood	High	Yes	Yes	No	No
Soft Maple, Cherry, Walnut	Medium	Yes	Yes	No	No
Elm, Sycamore, Gum	Medium	Medium	No	Medium	No
Aspen, Basswood, Cottonwood	Low	Yes	Yes	Medium	No
Chestnut, Poplar	Low	Yes	Yes	Medium	Yes
Southern Yellow Pine, Douglas Fir	High	Yes	Yes	Yes	No
Cypress, Redwood	Medium	Medium	Yes	Medium	No
White Cedar, Western Red Cedar, Eastern Red Cedar	Medium	Yes	Yes	Medium	Yes
White Pine, True Firs, Ponderosa Pine, Sugar Pine	Low	Medium	Yes	Medium	No
Tamarack, Larch	Medium	Yes	Yes	Medium	No
Spruce	Low	Yes	Yes	Medium	Yes

This discussion of our short firewood list shows that with very few fuel species, we still have enough variety to do whatever needs to be done with our stoves. The same is bound to be true in other areas of the country, even if the species of wood are entirely different. It pays to talk to old-timers about their preferences in woods, and to experiment to see which woods give the best results with any particular stove.

Chapter 7
Using Wood Stoves

Keeping a fire in a wood stove is like having a pet in the house with you. A fire needs your attention at regular intervals, and is in danger of either dying or running amok if your judgment slips. You have to feed it the right things at the appropriate times, and you have to carry its waste products out of the house. In return it will work for you, cooking your meals and heating your water and living space.

The kind of experience you have with your fire depends entirely upon your equipment and fuel and how you use them. Your fire may be a gentle, dependable, obedient servant, doing what you want it to do when you want it done; or it may be capricious and stubborn, misbehaving continually, a source of frequent irritation.

I'll never forget the time I watched a schoolteacher, new to the north, trying to fry meat on an oil-barrel wood stove in an Eskimo friend's house. "What's *wrong* with this thing?" she asked. "I just *filled* it." She was prodding the meat with a big fork, and I could tell by the absence of sound in the pan that the meat wasn't cooking. At the same time, she was shielding her thighs from the intensely hot sides of the stove.

I could see the bright glow of a fine bed of coals at the draft hole, and began to wonder why the frying pan wasn't heating up. So I got up, looked into the firebox and saw that she'd laid green birch on top of the coals. The birch shielded the stove top, so the coals radiated heat only to the sides of the stove.

I took the poker and slid the birch off the coals so that it would shield the sides of the stove rather than the top, and then I laid a couple of sticks of dry spruce in its place. The sides cooled right down, flames from the dry wood started heating the stove top and, shortly, the meat in the pan began to sizzle.

My friend had used the wrong wood in the wrong place at the wrong time and, naturally, the results were unsatisfactory. She simply hadn't been around wood stoves long enough to develop the feel needed to operate them properly. I began to think of all the other situations a person encounters in the course of a 24-hour period with a wood stove, and wondered if perhaps I couldn't put my own experience into words and help others learn to be more comfortable with their own woodburners. Then and there I began outlining this book. In the pages that follow I'll share every trick I know for getting maximum performance and enjoyment from a wood stove, as others have freely shared with me over the past ten years.

STARTING A FIRE. Fire-starting requires dry wood, so it is a good idea to have a box of kindling tucked away. Everybody has his own way of laying a new fire, and here is mine. Place two splits of dry wood on either side of the firebox, say 3 or 4 inches apart. If there is any old charcoal among the ashes, arrange it so it lies between the splits. Next lay some shredded paper on the charcoal. (Newspaper is ideal; avoid glossy paper such as in magazines.) Lay the kindling on top of the paper, and place a few small splits of wood on top of the kindling. Now light the paper and close the stove door. Open the draft just enough to encourage the fire without blowing it out. Once the stove is drawing well, add as much wood as the situation calls for.

Another way to kindle a fire is to use sawdust soaked in kerosene or waste crankcase oil. Place a couple of spoonfuls of the sawdust mixture among the kindling sticks, in place of the newspaper. Light the sawdust with a match, and you'll have an instant, trouble-free start-up. I should not have to add that gasoline or other explosive substances should *never* be used in stoves. The danger is obvious, yet I know a man who burned down a fine log house in this way. Also, never add kerosene to anything but a cold stove, since the heat may vaporize it, forming an explosive white cloud that could flash back in your face. The same goes for crankcase oil that is heavily contaminated with gasoline.

Purists like to start fires without resorting to newspaper or petroleum products. One good way to do so is to carve a fuzz stick from a piece of kindling (Figure 7.1). Put it in the firebox in place of the paper, and light the wood shavings with a match.

GETTING A STOVE TO DRAW. A stove draws because the warm gases produced by the fire are less dense than the cooler outside air and, consequently, tend to rise up the pipe. Once a fire is going and the stove is hot, the draft maintains itself; but occasionally a stove won't draw when it is being started up. This is especially true in the summertime, when there isn't much difference in temperature (and hence density) between inside and outside air.

I spent three winters in a little cabin at the base of a fairly high

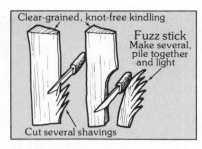

Clear-grained, knot-free kindling

Fuzz stick
Make several,
pile together
and light

Cut several shavings

Figure 7.1—How to make a fuzz stick
to use as a substitute for paper when
starting a fire.

bluff. On still, clear nights, cold, dense air from the tundra would cascade down the ravine behind the cabin and continue right on out to the river. I could always tell that a cold night was in store when the smoke curled out of the stovepipe, lay down flat, drifted horizontally across the roof, and then slid along the ground toward the riverbank. The cold air worked on my stovepipe all night, cooling the thin smoke from the banked fire so that it had little tendency to rise. If the stove happened to go out, I'd have trouble lighting it in the morning. As soon as I opened the firebox door, cold air would rush down the pipe, into the room.

The time-honored trick for getting a stove started in such a situation is to stuff a piece of newspaper loosely into the stovepipe and then light it. The paper will burn very quickly, sending a rush of warm air up the pipe. If the kindling in the firebox is lighted just before or just after the newspaper, the momentary draft will get it going. Heat from the budding fire will keep the draft going until the fire is well established.

In the stove arrangement I was using at the time, I usually stuck the newspaper into the pipe at the draft corrector, which was the handiest place. I also could have stuffed it way back at the far end of the firebox, near the exit to the flue. On other stoves, I've had to disconnect the elbow from the stove, put the paper into the pipe, light it, and then quickly reconnect the elbow. In some cases it might be necessary to insert the paper at a joint between two stovepipe sections, or to light it and stick it into the stovepipe from the roof, burning end down.

If a stove draws poorly even when hot, there is something wrong in the system. It may be that the pipe merely needs cleaning. Or it may be that the pipe is too short, and that adding a section or two will correct the problem. Switching to a pipe of larger diameter will also increase the draft, but this will involve some modification of the fixture where the pipe passes out of the house.

REKINDLING A SMALL FIRE. Sometimes a fire gets too low

to ignite regular firewood sticks, but if even a few glowing coals remain, it can be brought back to life with a little coddling. Place the coals in the center of the firebox, and lay a split of dry wood on either side. Place some kindling on the coals, and then add a few splits of firewood—just as in laying a new fire. Then *shut down the stove* (close the draft); too much draft at this stage will only cause the weak coals to burn themselves out without lighting the kindling.

With the draft closed, the wood will absorb enough heat from the coals to reach its kindling temperature. Then, when air is again admitted, the fire will spring to life. (Blowing lightly on the coals at this point may help establish the live flame.) If the cabin doesn't need the warmth just then, leave the stove shut down. The fire will ignite by itself later on.

HEATING: LIFE CYCLE OF A FIRE. I always think of a fire as a living thing; it seems to me to have a distinct life cycle. Let's suppose a fire is going well; it's in the prime of life, and heat output is at a maximum. In time, the wood will turn to charcoal, and the charcoal to ash. Without new fuel, the fire will die a natural death.

But by placing new wood on the fire while it is still fairly hot, we give the wheel another turn. At first, the fire cools down as the new wood absorbs heat. (With dry wood, this cooling phase may be so short as to be almost unnoticeable; with greener wood—especially if the stove is shut down tight—it may last for hours, even overnight.) Eventually the moisture is driven off, the wood reaches its kindling temperature, and the fire takes off, rejuvenated. As the fuel is consumed, heat output once more dwindles.

So wood heat is inherently uneven, rising and falling with each new charge of fuel. This unevenness—which is most noticeable in small cabins—can be counteracted by giving the fire a number of small feedings rather than a few large ones. That way the firebox always contains wood in several stages of the life cycle, and the ups and downs balance each other.

The interval between feedings may be long or short, depending on the stove, the fuel, the house and the weather. After developing a feeling for a stove, you'll know when it is time to take a look into the firebox. Sometimes you will close the door again without doing a thing; sometimes you will just stir the wood around a bit with the poker; sometimes you will draw the coals nearer to the draft and add more wood. In any case, when you've finished you'll know what the fire is doing and what you can expect of it.

Timing is always important. Dry wood is an agreeable fuel and will readily ignite, even if the fire has been neglected. But slower woods require that the stove be fed before the heat is actually needed. How long before depends on how long it takes the wood to reach its kindling temperature, which in turn depends upon its moisture and pitch content, physical size and hardness. By way of compensation, wood that is hard to get started is usually easy to control by shutting the draft; there is little risk of ruining your fire by adding such fuel before it is needed.

One good practice is to keep several types of wood on hand. When I chop wood, I try to include some dry, some half-dry and some punky wood in each batch, with some chunks split fine and others left large, even in the round. That way, I can always find just the wood I need for the firebox. If the fire is low, I'll reach for dry wood and small splits. If the fire is perking along nicely and I wish only to maintain it, I'll select larger chunks of half-dry.

MODERATING A FIRE. Wood stoves can be shut down by closing either the draft control or the damper, or both. Shutting the draft moderates the fire by shutting off the flow of oxygen. Shutting the damper produces the same effect by preventing the smoke from escaping up the pipe, for if smoke can't get out of the firebox, new air can't get in to take its place.

Although closing either the draft or the damper has the same effect on oxygen flow, the incidental results are somewhat different. If the draft is closed while the damper remains open, the live flame may die out altogether. The smoldering wood will give off a lot of smoke, meaning that a good deal of its heat value goes up the chimney in the form of unburned volatile substances. If the draft is left open while the damper is closed, on the other hand, the live flame will remain, and combustion will be much more complete.

TAMING A STOVE THAT WON'T SHUT DOWN. If I had to choose the most irritating kind of wood stove, it would be one that continues to throw off large amounts of heat even though I have tried to shut it down. Somehow I can tolerate a cold cabin in the knowledge that the stove will take the chill off quickly, but a hot room not only sets me on edge—it seems to take forever to cool down. And I find sleeping in a hot room impossible.

One winter I lived near Fairbanks in a small cabin that was heated by a cast-iron box stove. I don't know if all box stoves are as leaky as that one was, but I'll never willingly have another. Temperatures of -30 to -40° F dictated that I keep a fire overnight, but too often the stove would take off after only 2 or 3 hours. I'd wake up in a steamy room and see brilliant coals shining through the cracks between the various castings. The stove seemed to be leering at me, like some malevolent cast-iron pumpkin, and I hated it with a passion.

I'd jump out of bed, throw open the cabin door to let some fresh air in, lift one lid from the stove top, and pour water from the kettle onto the fire to cool it. A hissing cloud of steam and ashes would rush up at my face, making the whole cabin smell like a boiler room. Then I'd close the lid and go back to bed. Often the stove would take off a *second* time, and then I'd *really* douse it. Next morning the fire would be dead, the cabin would be cold, and I'd be cranky. On top of it all, my first chore of the day would be to kindle a new fire on a bed of soggy charcoal.

No doubt that stove would have been fine for a room five times the size of that particular cabin, or for a workshop or church that was heated only occasionally and never overnight. But it was definitely not the stove for my situation. In any case, this sort of thing is certainly not uncommon, and it pays to know how to deal with an intractable stove.

If you encounter a stove that runs on, even though both the draft and damper have been closed, there are ways to control the fire without adding to or replacing any of the equipment:

1. **Use less fuel.** Perhaps the problem is nothing more than unfamiliarity with a new stove or a new type of fuel. After a few fires that are too large to control, one generally develops a feel for the situation. If improper stoking of the stove is at fault, some of the hints on keeping a small fire (later in this chapter) may help. If the problem goes deeper than that, escalate. Read on.

2. **Use different fuel.** Sometimes switching to a slower-burning fuel will be enough to moderate a stove that tends to go out of control. For me, this means switching from dry spruce to half-dry spruce, alder or birch. In a different case, though, these woods could easily aggravate the problem. After a time-lag, they might themselves take off, producing a *really* intense fire that could not be controlled.

3. **Remove fuel.** Zany as it may sound, there have been times when I have done this—usually when bread-making has fallen behind schedule and my wife, Manya, has found it necessary to bake in the evening. As soon as the bread comes out of the oven, I yank some of the wood from the firebox with a pair of tongs, place it in an empty 5-gallon can, carry it quickly outside, and dump it on the snow. (The charred wood goes back into the stove the next morning.) Then I use the remaining coals to set the fire for overnight, even if it is an hour or two until bedtime. The stove and the room both cool gradually, so that we can sleep comfortably.

4. **Add fuel.** A good stove, as well as an intractable one, will often run on once the fire has reached the charcoal stage, because the coals radiate surprising amounts of heat even with a minimum of oxygen. The simplest way to moderate a charcoal fire is to lay some new fuel on the coals and shut the stove down again. Naturally, a moister wood is best, since it takes longer to reach its kindling temperature. The new wood will absorb a lot of heat from the coals in the meantime—heat that otherwise would have been radiating into the room. By the time the new fuel finally takes off, the room ought to be ready for the extra heat. If it's not, the problem worsens.

5. **Add water.** Throwing water on a fire, from the standpoint of a wood-stove purist, is an inelegant thing to do. It's also very effective. But it is a bad sign; heavy reliance on this technique indicates that something is not right with the system and that fundamental changes are in order.

6. **Seal off the coals.** One of my favorite tricks for cooling a fire is to lay paper over it. News magazines and mail-order catalogs are just right, since the glossy paper produces a flaky, smothering ash that continues to seal the coals long after the paper is carbonized. (This is why magazines can foul a fire so badly when incinerated in a wood stove.)

    When it's time to revive the fire, simply stir around with a poker and lift the remaining coals to the surface. They'll be half black, half red, and strangely inactive, so it sometimes takes a bit of kindling or good wood to get a hot fire going again.

    Ashes can also be used to seal off the coals. A friend of mine, who grew up in the country, told me that his mother kept an overnight fire in her big wood range by putting ashes on top of a charge of wood. With a shake of the grate in the morning, the ashes sifted away from the coals and the fire was reborn.

7. **Seal the draft hole.** Perhaps the stove runs on because the draft fixture is leaky. With many stoves it is possible to rake ashes forward and cover the draft hole completely. In the morning the opening can be unplugged with the poker or a piece of wire. Any ashes that fall can be caught in the ash can.

8. **Seal the stove.** Many stoves can benefit from an application of fireplace putty or asbestos chinking to the cracks. On some units the cracks can be welded or brazed shut.

9. **Use a door** *piñya*. On many stoves the main source of air leakage is the stoke-hole door. A simple foil door closure pad, or *piñya* (see Chapter 5), will quite effectively seal off leaks in many types of stoves. Intense heat will destroy the foil fairly quickly, so it is good to moderate the fire in some other way before sealing off the door with the *piñya*.
10. **Fix the door.** If the stoke-hole door itself is at fault, it may be possible to remove it, heat it up, and pound it back into its original shape, thus sealing the air leaks that are causing the problem.

Sometimes a stove runs on simply because it is connected to a stovepipe that provides too much draft. Wind blowing across the top of an open stovepipe or chimney, excessive stovepipe length or diameter, and strong indoor-outdoor temperature differentials can all contribute to excessive draft.

There are two approaches to this problem. One is to make structural modifications that reduce the draft—for example, installing an anti-wind stovepipe cap, or shifting to a smaller or shorter pipe. The other is to leave the piping alone, but spoil the draft by letting it pull air into the pipe directly from the room rather than through the firebox.

There are many ways to do this. Some stoves (notably wood ranges) have little cleanout doors designed to give access to the smoke passageways. Any of these can be left open to act as spoilers. My neighbor accomplishes the same thing by sliding his airtight heater forward a bit, creating a spoiler opening in the joint where the horizontal pipe from the stove joins the tee in the main stovepipe. Or the lids in the surface of a wood range can be tilted so that they remain partially open.

But to my mind the most versatile spoiler of all is a draft corrector (see Chapter 4). If the swiveling flap is held shut with a simple spring-type clothespin clamped to the rim, the corrector is effectively taken out of the system, and the full draft pulls at the firebox. With the pin shifted to the flap so that it is jammed in the wide open position, most of the draft pulls room air into the pipe; this should tame almost any stove (Figure 7.2).

It is worth noting that any air that goes up the draft corrector must be replaced by new air entering the room. Ordinarily the replacement air comes into the house through cracks around doors and windows, so the price of controlling an intractable stove may be drafts and a cold floor. With the addition of a couple of simple stovepipe fixtures, however, these problems can be eliminated. In the October, 1975 issue of *Organic Gardening and Farming*, Tom

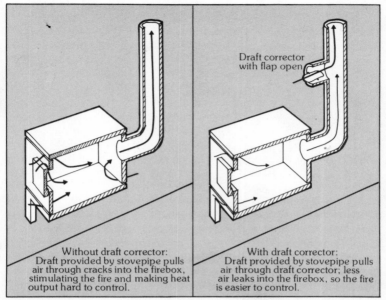

Draft corrector
with flap open

Without draft corrector:
Draft provided by stovepipe pulls
air through cracks into the firebox,
stimulating the fire and making heat
output hard to control.

With draft corrector:
Draft provided by stovepipe pulls
air through draft corrector; less
air leaks into the firebox, so the fire
is easier to control.

Figure 7.2—How to use a draft corrector as a spoiler in order to make the fire burn more slowly.

and Peggy Blunt described how they tamed their stove without sacrificing comfort.

The Blunts were having trouble shutting down their box stove—the same kind that gave me so much trouble that winter near Fairbanks. Their solution was to install a draft corrector at the first section of stovepipe leading from the top of the stove. Then they removed the ring holding the swiveling flap, and inserted an elbow in its place. Next, they added a joint of stovepipe that ran downward to within 3 inches of the floor, and inserted the swiveling flap in the bottom of the pipe. Finally, they cut a 6 inch hole in the floor beneath the stove (Figure 7.3).

The operation of this system is exactly the same as that of a conventionally mounted draft corrector, except that the flap is manually controlled and cooler air from the floor (rather than warmer air from a higher level) is drawn into the stovepipe. To replace it, preheated air from the crawl space beneath the floor enters the room through the hole under the stove. The Blunts say that cold-air leakage around their doors and windows has stopped since they installed this simple system.

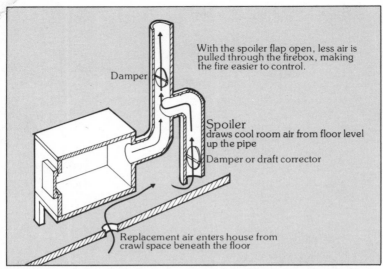

With the spoiler flap open, less air is pulled through the firebox, making the fire easier to control.

Damper

Spoiler
draws cool room air from floor level up the pipe

Damper or draft corrector

Replacement air enters house from crawl space beneath the floor

Figure 7.3—The Blunts' draft-spoiler system. A draft corrector is installed in the first vertical section of stovepipe leading from the stove, an elbow replacing the swiveling flap. A joint of stovepipe runs to within 3 inches of the floor and the swiveling flap or a damper is inserted in the bottom of the pipe. Replacement air enters through a hole cut in the floor under the stove.

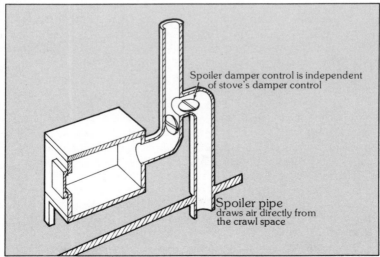

Spoiler damper control is independent of stove's damper control

Spoiler pipe
draws air directly from the crawl space

Figure 7.4—A refinement of the draft spoiler in Figure 7.3. This system is independent of the stove damper, and no air is drawn through the room.

Figure 7.4 shows a refinement of this system that might be even more effective. The draft corrector is placed *above* the first section of stovepipe, rather than directly on the stove, making the operation of the air by-pass system independent of the stove damper. With the extender pipe run directly into the crawl space, no room air at all is drawn away through the bypass. Since the end of the pipe is out of reach beneath the floor, the swiveling flap is unnecessary, and a simple tee rather than a draft corrector can be used. A second damper, placed close to the junction of the pipe sections for convenience, is used to control the bypass air.

HOLDING A FIRE OVERNIGHT. This is the acid test of a wood stove's manageability. Any old metal box will give out heat in the daytime, but it takes some thought to construct a stove that can be closed tightly enough to maintain the fire without attention for eight hours or more. Some commercial models are so well constructed that one need only add wood at bedtime and set an automatic thermostat to be assured of all-night warmth and a fine fire in the morning. Lesser stoves, with a little coddling, can be made to perform similarly.

Living in an extreme climate, I have to walk a thin line between two evils when setting an overnight fire. If I lean too far toward the cold side and apply all the tricks, the fire may actually die, even though the firebox is full of wood. In the morning both the stove and the cabin will be cold. Even worse, if I ease up too much on my fire-holding techniques, the fire may take off in the wee hours and drive us from under the covers. But with good equipment and a little experience, there's no reason not to wake up and find the fire in excellent condition, and the cabin just comfortably cool.

I've never counted how many times in our seven-month winter I need to use a match on our homemade stove, but it can't be many. I do remember that we once returned to the cabin on the 15th of March, following a long trip. I used one match that morning to start the fire, and the very same fire was still going on April 29, the morning we left for spring camp. Similarly, brochures for some of the better commercial models promise that one need only "build only two or three fires a winter." It's true.

The fundamental goal of setting an overnight fire is to be able to get the fire going the next morning without rekindling. With a good stove, properly set, it's not at all unusual to get up after a night's sleep and have a dormant fire roaring again in 60 seconds (Figure 7.5). Assuming a stove is reasonably airtight, there are four steps in setting an overnight fire:

1. Begin with the right quantity of coals. Try to regulate the

Figure 7.5—A fire can be held over-night in any reasonably tight stove. This fire is just taking off after lying dormant for more than 8 hours. Smoke is rising and there are brilliant, hot coals under the logs on the right. The somewhat leaky door had been sealed all night with a foil closure pad.

evening feedings of the fire in such a way that there will be enough glowing coals at bedtime to ignite the overnight charge of wood with certainty, but not so many that the fire takes off too soon. If the coal bed happens to be too rich when you are ready to set the fire, it can be weakened by laying some catalog or magazine paper over it. If the coals are too skimpy, add kindling to the base of the overnight charge.

2. **Select the right wood.** Hardwoods hold a fire longer than softwoods; large chunks hold longer than small pieces; wood still "in the round" holds longer than split wood; wood that is at all green holds longer than seasoned wood; and wood freshly brought in from the cold holds longer than wood that is warm from storage indoors. The wood must be chosen to match the characteristics of the stove and the quantity and quality of the coals remaining in the firebox. The only way to learn how to choose the wood is through experience with a particular stove and local fuels.

3. **Shut down tight.** The draft control and the stoke-hole door must be closed, of course. Depending on the inherent airtightness of the stove, exclude oxygen by any or all of the following means: close the damper; seal the draft opening with ashes; lay paper over the coals and wood; wrap each piece of wood in paper; seal the stoke-hole door with aluminum foil.

4. **Spoil the draft.** Use any of the techniques just given for taming a stove that won't shut down.

Once basic fire-setting techniques have been mastered, it is taken for granted that there will be fire in the stove 8 or 10 hours after it is set. The next refinement is to set the fire so that it not only holds till morning, but gives off the desired amount of heat through the night.

For example, when the weather is especially warm (zero or above), an overnight fire is optional in our cabin. At such times I often set the fire to go out—that is, I select wood that will not quite be ignited by the remaining coals. Heat output is minimal, and in the morning the fire is dead. But by that time the charred wood has been dried out by the residual heat of the firebox, and can be kindled by nothing more than a few pieces of paper and a match.

In cold weather (down to -30°F), I set the fire in the normal way. The coals just maintain themselves, and heat output through the night is low. In the morning, most of the wood is still in the firebox, completely dried out and heat soaked. Ample coals remain, so the whole thing takes right off as soon as the stove is opened up.

In severe weather (-30 to -50°F), I slack off a bit on fire-holding techniques so that heat output at night will be moderate. By morning most of the wood is gone, but there are plenty of coals at the back of the stove to get the fire going without difficulty.

In extreme weather (-50°F or colder) I set the fire to last only about 4 hours so that heat output will be appreciable. Then, just before bedtime, I drink a couple of glasses of water. That way, I am sure to get up in the middle of the night, at which time I can refill the firebox and set the fire for another 4 hours or so.

KEEPING A SMALL FIRE. Toward spring, as the weather moderates, I keep a smaller and smaller fire until only two sticks of wood remain in the firebox, with a few coals between them. The two pieces of wood, lying side by side, reflect heat back and forth, and so keep each other going. When one of them crumbles into coals, I replace it with a fresh stick.

For an even smaller fire, I use a slow type of wood for one of the two sticks. It takes a long time for the slow stick to soak up heat and dry out, but its surface chars, and serves as a heat reflector to keep the other, drier stick burning.

Another way to keep a small fire is to push the coals up against one side of the firebox and lay a single stick of firewood against them. If the coals begin to fade, a stick or two of kindling will replenish them. To go even smaller, one can use shorter and shorter wood. For example, my present stove will take wood up to 23 inches in length, but in spring and summer I sometimes use wood only 6 to 8 inches long. By that time it's a tossup whether it's more trouble to keep the tiny fire going, or to let it die and rekindle another when needed.

INCINERATING. Until America devises a system for reducing solid waste and recycling what's left, we might as well salvage at least the energy content by burning the combustible portions in our wood stoves. Wastepaper, cardboard, and scrap lumber can all contribute to the household heat budget while lessening the burden on the sanitation department.

One Way to Set an Overnight Fire

Different stoves require different strategies for setting fires that will last all night. Here is how I hold a fire in my homemade sheet-steel Super Yukon stove:

1. Let the fire die down in the evening so that only coals remain at bedtime.
2. Push the coals to the back of the firebox, and rake ashes forward to seal the draft.
3. Lay a split of half-dry spruce on either side of the coals. If there are too many or too few coals, use a stick of greenish or dry wood, respectively, on one side.
4. Place a smaller split of wood on top of the coals, between the two larger splits. This completes the foundation—the heart of the fire (Figure 7.6, Drawing A). If it behaves as it should, the rest of the fire will take care of itself.
5. Lay paper over the entire foundation, overlapping the various sections generously to make a good seal. Use magazine or glossy catalog paper, five to ten pages thick. Tuck the paper down around the front of the foundation, so that the wood is encased in a chamber which is open only at the rear.
6. Add another round of splits. These may be fairly low-quality, moist wood, since the slow heat of the smoldering foundation in the chamber below will dry them out by morning. If only drier wood is available, lay paper over this round too, so that it won't ignite too soon.
7. Lay a wall of paper against the front of the whole stack of wood, just inside the door.
8. Put a foil closure pad over the door opening, and close the door on it.
9. Close the damper. The fire is now set (Figure 7.6, Drawing B).

Remember, though, that the smell of burning garbage can be a real nuisance. Wet trash is especially offensive, because it smolders for a long time. Burn trash on a good hot fire so the job is done quickly and the smoke is consumed in the flames. Give a thought to the wind direction, too, if you plan to be working outside or if you have near neighbors.

10. In the morning, if all goes as it should, the papers inside the door will be charred but intact, the foundation logs will have been converted in varying degree to glowing charcoal, and the upper logs will be dried out and ready to go. Open the damper, open the door, remove the foil, punch through the papers with the poker, and stir the fire around a bit to break up the paper ash over the foundation. Clear the ashes away from the draft and open it. Shut the door. The fire will now take off.

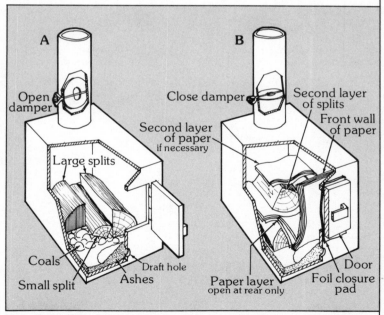

Figure 7.6—Two of the stages in setting an overnight fire. In Drawing A the foundation is laid. In Drawing B it is all tucked in and the damper is closed.

What To Do With Ashes

Looking at things ecologically, ashes belong on the ground. By sprinkling ashes on the soil in the forest or woodlot, we complete one of nature's great cycles. The mineral substances in the ashes are available to make new wood, and all we've really taken out of the forest is renewable solar energy.

Here are some other uses for wood ashes:

1. **Fertilizing the garden.** Wood ashes contain significant amounts of several minerals essential to the healthy growth of plants. They also contain potash, which is useful for neutralizing excess acidity in some soils. It is best, however, to check the gardening books before applying wood ashes, since some plants do best in soils that are on the acid side. Garden supply houses sell inexpensive kits for determining whether soil is acid or alkaline.

   Wood ashes should be stored in a dry place if they are to be used as fertilizer, because water will leach away several important minerals. To enrich the ashes even further, burn bones from the table in the stove. They will crumble to powder, adding calcium, phosphorus and other elements to the ashes.

2. **Making alkali.** Soap is made from fat and lye. In the old days, lye was made by trickling water through wood ashes and boiling down the resulting liquor to concentrate the alkali. For best results, use rain or snow water (which has minimal mineral content) and boil it first (to remove carbon dioxide). Do not use iron or aluminum vessels at any stage of the process, because they are affected by alkalis.

3. **Melting snow.** A thin layer of wood ashes on snow will encourage more rapid melting, since the dark ashes absorb sunlight. This is a handy trick for clearing the garden and allowing the sun to warm the bare earth a bit sooner in the springtime.

4. **Deodorizing outhouses.** A layer of ashes forms a physical barrier to odor, and the alkalinity interferes with bacterial action and the growth of fly larvae. For best results, keep a can of ashes right inside the privy and apply a small amount daily.

Chapter 8
Cooking With Wood Stoves

Irma Rombauer and Marion Becker, in their excellent book, *Joy of Cooking,* lament "the passing of the back of the stove," which was ideal for slowly cooking soups, stews, and many other dishes which benefit from long, gentle simmering. Those of us who still cook on wood stoves know exactly what they mean. The following tips are based on more than ten years' experience in wood-stove cookery:

FRYING. This is a test of a good cookstove. If you can do a good job of frying without overheating the room, you either have a good cookstove or a very large room. Whenever you want to fry something with a minimum of unwanted heat, anticipate. Place good wood on the coals, and then shut down the stove so the fuel can soak up heat. Place the frying pan on the cooking surface and let it preheat. When the wood has reached its take-off point and the pan is hot, open the draft and damper and let the fire go. Shift the pan to hotter or cooler parts of the stove top, as the situation requires. (With some stoves it is possible to find the hot spots by peeking into the firebox to see where the flames are licking the stove top.)

Some cooking utensils can benefit from a coat of black stove enamel if they are going to be used on a wood stove. I remember one time when I tried to cook sourdough hotcakes in a brand-new aluminum frying pan. The hotcakes simply sat there and dried out without browning, even though the stove top turned red hot underneath the pan. I reasoned that the pan's shiny bottom was reflecting most of the heat back to the stove top rather than absorbing it. So I bought a pint of Black Silk Stove Enamel and painted the bottom of the frying pan.

The next time I used the pan, the results were perfect: golden-brown hotcakes, no red-hot stove top. The blackened pan absorbed the heat rather than reflecting it. Encouraged by this success, I painted the bottom of *every* vessel that *ever* touched the stove—the pots, pans, kettles, dishpans, wash basins and snow-melting buckets (Figure 8.1). The trick is well worth remembering. Roughen the bottom of the vessel with sandpaper before painting it, use two coats, and let it dry for 24 hours in a warm place before using. And be sure to use the stove *enamel,* not the *polish.*

Figure 8.1—Applying a coat of stove enamel to the bottom of a water-heating can with a cotton-tipped swab. The black surface will absorb heat much more efficiently than the shiny, untreated metal.

A real virtuoso performance is required to make popcorn on a wood stove. To do this you need a really hot frying fire, for if the heat is too low, the kernels will dry out, and without moisture, they cannot develop the steam pressure required for proper popping. The result is a pan full of dried-out, unpopped "grannies." At the same time, a fire that is too hot can cause the kernels to pop prematurely, when only the outer layers are heated up properly, giving undersized, deformed kernels. But this can be allowed for by lifting the pan off the stove top slightly and shaking vigorously.

To pop corn on my first little oil-barrel stove, I'd first lay a generous handful of kindling on top of the coals, and then shut the stove down tight. While the wood was soaking up heat, I'd have the popcorn pot and the oil heating on the stove top. When the wood was ready, I'd open the draft and damper and let the fire go. The kindling would immediately take off, and soon there'd be a red spot on the top of the stove—something I always avoided under more normal conditions. I'd keep the pot as close to the red spot as necessary for proper popping, and then quench the pot quickly in the wash basin, so that the bottom layers of popcorn wouldn't burn. While the pot cooled, I'd lay a charge of wood on the coals (for later), shut the stove down again, and then enjoy the popcorn.

ROASTING. Many different styles of roasting pans are on the market—aluminum or enameled steel, heavy or light gauge, flat or round bottomed, large or small. All work well with wood stoves, either on the stove top or in the oven. Roasting recipes often call for the meat to be seared first, in order to seal in the juices. For this step, arrange a frying fire. Then moderate it to a heating fire for the long, slow roasting process. To keep the heat steady, add small amounts of firewood fairly often rather than a few big charges at longer intervals.

Proper roasting on the top of a wood stove, to my mind, requires more attention than any other type of cooking. If the pan gets too hot, the juices dry up and the meat burns. If the pan is not hot enough, the juices accumulate until the meat is steaming rather than roasting. Either way, the flavor changes markedly.

Sound is the best indication as to the correctness of the heat. Popping and spattering indicate that the pan is too hot and the juices are drying up, while a slow bubbling indicates that the pan is too cool and juices are accumulating. Somewhere in between is the gentle, pleasing sound of a roast cooking just the way it should. I always like to do away with extraneous noise when the roaster is on, in order to tune in to the sounds of the cooking meat. That way, I can add wood, or close the damper, or shift the roaster to a different part of the stove top, and be assured that the roast will turn out just right.

SIMMERING. This is where a wood stove really comes into its own. Even some heaters that aren't much good at most kinds of cooking can produce just the right sort of heat for simmering.

Simmering requires the right vessel. I prefer a 12-quart stock pot with a good cover. For soups, the cover may be left closed, but for stews, I like to keep the lid open slightly. I use a repair link from a chain to prop the lid open about a quarter of an inch at one side, but almost anything will do, as long as it holds the lid open far enough to prevent a build-up of water vapor.

Proper heat is also essential to simmering because, as the authors of *Joy of Cooking* point out, "a stew boiled is a stew spoiled." The top of a wood stove is apt to heat up and cool down as each charge of wood goes through its life cycle, and it only takes a few minutes at the boiling point to ruin a good dish. A slowly simmered pot of meat and bones, for example, will give a rich, delicious broth with lots of suspended solids to give it body. Boiling causes the solids to clump and sink to the bottom, leaving behind a clear and far less tasty broth. (You can smell a boiled broth pot as soon as you walk into the room.)

Rather than take a chance on having the broth spoiled by an unexpected surge of stove-top heat, I always place the pot on a trivet, either right at the outset or as soon as the contents have reached the cooking temperature. Whenever I feed the fire, I check the temperature of the pot by touching it lightly with the back of my fingers. A low simmer is hot enough that the skin can't be left in contact with the metal, but not so hot that it is at all uncomfortable to touch the pot briefly to make the test. According to Rombauer and Becker, low simmering temperatures range from 130 to 135°F, a heat level that the French refer to as "making the pot smile." I can understand why.

Sometimes a simmering temperature can be too *low*. Once I left a good soup to simmer all night. With the stove shut down, the pot was just warm enough for the rapid incubation of bacteria, and the soup fermented. It was a total loss.

PRESSURE COOKING. The principle behind pressure cooking is that the boiling point of water rises with increased pressure. At sea-level atmospheric pressure water boils at 212°F, while at 15 pounds additional pressure—the operating range of most pressure pots—the boiling point is 250°F. The chief advantage of pressure cookery is that food cooks much faster at the higher temperatures. Stew meat, for example, will be tender after cooking only 15 minutes.

Once the food has been placed in the pressure cooker, a small amount of water is added to prevent scorching and provide steam, and the lid is fastened in place. The pot is then brought quickly to a boil. For the first few minutes the vent is left open so the steam can sweep air out of the vessel. This eliminates oxygen, preventing it from degrading the nutrients and flavor of the food. It also allows efficient transfer of heat from the bottom of the pot to the contents by superheated steam during the cooking period.

When the emerging steam seems to be pure water vapor, the regulator is set in place. The pressure within the pot immediately begins to rise, and at 15 pounds has enough force to lift the regulator off its seat so that some steam can escape. The heat is then adjusted so that the regulator puffs lightly. (Some models have pressure gauges instead of regulators, in which case the heat is adjusted to maintain the dial at the proper level.)

When full pressure is reached, the cooking period begins. Pressure is maintained for the number of minutes called for in the recipe, and then the pot is either taken off the stove and allowed to cool by itself or it is quenched quickly under cold water.

Timing is all-important in pressure cookery. The food cooks all through the period of pressure build-up, and recipe books assume that this period will be brief. If pressure build-up is slow, the cooking time at full pressure needs to be reduced correspondingly, or the food will be cooked to death.

So the challenge of wood-stove pressure cookery is to have the stove top hot enough to bring the pot to full pressure in the shortest possible time, and then to maintain that pressure throughout the cooking period. A good wood range will certainly be up to the challenge, particularly if one of the lids over the firebox is removed and the pot is set right in the opening, where the fire can touch it directly. But many other stoves will not measure up. For example, my present stove heats the cabin too much if fired up for proper pressure cookery, so I generally use the pressure pot on the gasoline camp stove. That way nothing comes out overcooked.

TOASTING. Wood stoves turn out fine toast. Place the bread on a dry skillet, a piece of aluminum foil, or directly on the stove top. Shop around for just the right temperature, and turn the bread as often as necessary. This is also a good way to freshen up crackers and hardtack that have picked up moisture from the air and started tasting old. The stove top needn't be very hot to crisp them nicely; ideally, they shouldn't change color at all.

CHARCOAL COOKING. When we go out fighting forest fires in the summer fire season, the Bureau of Land Management feeds us on C-rations for 6½ days a week, and then flies out a batch of steaks for Sunday dinner. We wrap the meat in aluminum foil and cook it in the coals from the campfire. I remember one dark November evening when one of my Eskimo friends, nostalgic for summertime, wrapped a caribou steak in foil and set it on the coals right inside his oil-barrel wood stove. The results were excellent.

Anybody who uses a wood stove has a source of charcoal always at hand. For cooking on a *hibachi* (Japanese charcoal grill), one must only lift the glowing coals from the firebox with a pair of tongs—no need for kindling or charcoal starter, and no waiting. Remember, though, that charcoal produces a certain amount of carbon monoxide as it burns, so it is necessary to have adequate ventilation and to flip the coals back into the firebox as soon as the meal is cooked.

Charcoal can also be stored for later use. Dead coals from a cold stove can be stored safely in a metal container for use the next time the grill is fired up. Live coals can be placed on a piece of heavy metal (even the stove top), well separated; they will radiate so much heat away that they will soon die out. (Especially vigorous coals may require a few drops of water.) It is best to pack the charcoal away by hand, so that there will be no chance of mixing a live coal with the dead ones. A single live spot on one coal might turn the whole storage can into a *hibachi*.

Figure 8.2 — Wood-stove cookery: 12-quart stock pot, tea pot and heavy frying pan on the tent stove.

BAKING. The challenge of baking on a wood stove is to manipulate the draft, damper, smoke flap, size of wood, type of wood, and feeding interval to maintain the oven at a high, steady temperature throughout a prolonged baking period. Other than a small oven thermometer, wood stoves have no dials to tell you how to proceed. Nevertheless, like any other type of wood-stove cookery, baking can be done beautifully by feel alone.

Whether the baking is to be done in a built-in oven, a stovepipe oven or a stove-top oven, a bed of glowing coals will not by itself produce the hot, moving gases that are necessary for proper temperature. Baking requires fresh wood and hot, live flames to carry the heat. So lay a good fire, and preheat the oven so that it is near the desired temperature when the baking pans go in. Then give the fire small charges of wood at regular intervals throughout the baking period.

It is important to anticipate: A rising oven will continue to get hotter even after the stove has been shut down, so the draft or damper may have to be closed before the thermometer indicates that the desired temperature has been reached. Likewise, a falling oven will continue to cool for a while even after more wood has been added to the firebox, so it may be necessary to refuel even though the thermometer registers just the right temperature.

Stoves with built-in ovens are usually well insulated, so the heat goes into the oven and not into the room. Stovepipe ovens, by contrast, are usually uninsulated, so the heat which escapes through the oven's outer shell is added to the considerable heat put out by the hot baking fire in the stove itself. Some planning may be needed if the house is not to become overheated.

Here is the routine Manya uses for baking in our stovepipe oven:
1. When the dough is almost ready to bake, shove all the coals to the back of the stove, directly beneath the outlet to the stovepipe. Lay one or two splits of slow wood against the side of the firebox to shade it from the heat and to crowd the coals together.
2. Lay small, short sticks of fast dry wood on the coals. The idea is to have a small, intense fire just beneath the flue opening, so that the flames can travel directly up the pipe to the oven without heating much of the stove top.
3. Check the temperature in the oven often to keep track of how fast the oven is heating up. When the thermometer registers about 75 or 100°F below the desired baking temperature, moderate the fire to allow for the time-lag characteristic of the heavy oven.
4. A few minutes later, when the temperature is about right, put the pans into the oven. (I say "about right" because this whole process is very approximate.)
5. Feed the fire regularly throughout the baking period. This is a good time to use up scrap cardboard, since it produces quick, hot flames but no coals. Check the temperature often, and turn the pans around if they are cooking more on one end than on the other. Shift them from the top to the bottom shelf if necessary.
6. When the baking is finished, lay some slow wood on the remaining coals and shut the stove down. Both the stove and the room can then cool to normal temperatures again.

In the days before we had the stovepipe oven, Manya baked in a little stove-top oven made from two 5-gallon cans, one inside the other (see Chapter 20). She has also used the commercial kind. Either way, there is no choice but to heat up the entire stove. One way of reducing the amount of excess heat thrown off into the room is to lay some green wood or other slow fuel against the sides of the firebox to shield them, letting most of the heat escape through the stove top. A kettle or 5-gallon can of water on the free portion of the stove top will also help, absorbing some of the excess heat during the baking period, and releasing it slowly later on. Another trick is to bake first thing in the morning, when the room is coolest and the extra heat is needed most.

Even without an oven of any kind, you don't have to go without baked goods. Most baking can be done right on the stove top, in a heavy frying pan with a good lid. Cook pan biscuits either covered or uncovered, and turn them once with a fork or spatula. For large, round, flat loaves of bread, cook the dough (covered) until it's almost done, then slide it out onto the inside of the lid and turn it back into the pan with the uncooked side down. (Use a well-seasoned pan so that the dough won't stick.) Keep cakes and other baked goods too delicate to be turned over tightly covered, use a lower heat, and cook correspondingly longer.

Some people use the old campfire trick of baking in a Dutch oven right in the coals. This is an especially good method to use with top-loading airtight heaters. (Although smaller airtights are sometimes suitable for use with a stove-top oven, the larger models throw off far too much heat from the sides to be used in this way, so the Dutch-oven method is better.) With practice, one gets a feeling for the intensity of heat generated by a given bed of coals and for the time and temperature requirements of any particular dough. Our neighbor has used this method for years, and turns out some really amazing breads and cakes—showing that as long as you have fire, there's no reason not to have baked goods, too.

Chapter 9
Stove Safety

Anybody who depends on a wood stove for heat is bound to be conscious of the danger of fire, but perhaps we are more than ordinarily concerned here in the North. We have lived in isolated situations where, had a fire destroyed our one-room cabin, we could have been left outdoors in air -40°F or colder, possibly lightly clad and barefoot, with a mile and a half to travel through deep snow to the nearest neighbor.

This sort of prospect naturally gives a person certain ideas on wood-stove safety. But in order to flesh out my own personal list of safety measures, I wrote to men of wider experience—fire-fighting professionals—for their thoughts. Mr. Gordon Brunton, Regional Fire Marshal for the State of Alaska, offered these suggestions:

STOVE LOCATION AND INSTALLATION

1. Locate the stove where it cannot block fire escape.
2. Locate the stove a safe distance from walls, furniture and other combustibles.
3. Protect wood floors under stoves with a ventilated air space, insulation and/or a non-combustible material.
4. Be sure that the stove is firmly positioned.
5. Install flues or stovepipes with non-combustible collars, and space them at least 6 inches from any combustible materials. Use straight, short runs of stovepipe. Avoid horizontal runs and multiple elbows.
6. Stack robbers are a source of trouble as they soot up easily, presenting a point for carbon stack fires.
7. Be sure that the stovepipe extends far enough above the roof to draw properly. The roof should be of fire-retardant material.

STOVE USE

1. Always have a plan for emergency escape.
2. Keep all combustibles such as clothing, curtains, boxes and firewood a safe distance from the stove.

3. Remember that green firewood, when burned, can cause corrosive deposits to form in the stove and flue. These can cause the metal to deteriorate.
4. Use extreme care in cooking on any type of stove. Grease is a flammable liquid; it should never be allowed to get too hot, and should be cleaned up if spilled around the stove. Never let a pot, pan or kettle boil dry. The food in it could burn, or the pot could melt, unbalance, and fall off the stove onto a combustible surface.
5. Keep a metal screen firmly in front of any open stoves or fireplaces to prevent sparks from falling on combustibles.

STOVE MAINTENANCE
1. Carefully examine the stove and flue periodically for signs of deterioration. Replace any defective parts or equipment.
2. When cleaning ashes from the stove, place them in a covered metal container outdoors.
3. Remember that it is cheaper to replace a worn stovepipe than the whole house.

Mr. Brunton refers to the problem of stack fires, and we should consider this insidious hazard in some detail. Burning wood gives off a wide variety of volatile organic chemicals. Some of these substances are consumed in the flames, some escape to the atmosphere with the smoke, and—here is the problem—some condense in the cooler regions of the stovepipe, along with water vapor. The condensate, a dark, watery liquid with a pungent odor, is commonly known as "creosote." (Technically, this is a misnomer; the creosotes commonly used as wood preservatives are distillates of coal tar and wood tar.)

As the creosote trickles back down the inside of the stovepipe, it reaches progressively warmer environments, and the more volatile fractions are again driven off. Complex chemical reactions among the remaining compounds yield substances which can no longer be evaporated by the heat of the flue. Over a period of time, the inside of the pipe becomes encrusted with a hard, black, tenacious layer that can easily reach a thickness of a quarter of an inch or more. Since the deposits shrink when they dry, curly flakes continually peel off and fall down the pipe to the nearest horizontal surface (elbow, oven), where they lie like a pile of tinder-dry leaves or wood chips.

Stack deposits, being organic in nature, are composed largely of carbon, and so are readily combustible. The chips may accumulate unnoticed over a period of weeks or months, and then ignite when, as it occasionally does, the stack temperature rises above its usual range. Once a stack fire gets started, it tends to perpetuate and intensify itself. Hot gases produced by the burning chips rush up the stovepipe, increasing the draft and pulling still more oxygen to the fire. The increased draft also stimulates the main fire in the firebox, further elevating the temperature of the flue gases and the stovepipe. In some installations, the suction produced by a stack fire is so strong that the fire keeps on raging even if the draft control and the damper are completely closed. The stovepipe can glow red, igniting walls or ceiling, and a shower of sparks can rain down onto the roof.

There are several ways to avoid this danger. One is to strive for complete combustion within the firebox. If the various compounds that make up creosote are burned there, nothing but water vapor will be left to condense inside the stovepipe.

Unfortunately, some stoves are designed in such a way that complete combustion rarely occurs. Further, those that have secondary air inlets, designed to help burn the smoke, may still give off unburned volatiles when operated at low temperatures.

Another way to minimize the formation of stack deposits is to try to minimize condensation within the piping, so that the creosote-producing substances remain in the vapor state all the way to the atmosphere. It is very tempting, in the search for wood-stove efficiency, to try to squeeze every bit of waste heat from the flue gases before they escape to the atmosphere. We install stack robbers, leave oven doors ajar, and so on. Some people even advocate running the stovepipe clear across the room just below the ceiling in order to capture the most heat from the smoke.

The problem is that heat cannot be withdrawn from any part of the piping without lowering the temperature at that point and at every point beyond. Lowered temperature means increased condensation, increased carbon build-up and increased danger of stack fires. Thus, beyond a certain point, waste heat is not waste at all—it is necessary for keeping the stovepipe warm enough to minimize condensation.

According to this line of reasoning, stovepipes should be insulated, so that the gases stay hot all the way to the atmosphere. The brochures of the Riteway Company indicate that condensation becomes a problem when the stack temperature falls below 250°F. The thermostatic control system on the Vermont Woodstove Company's DownDrafter is designed to maintain the stack temperature not lower than 300 to 400°F.

Another approach to the creosote problem is to be conscientious in selecting fuel woods. Hardwoods produce less creosote than softwoods, and seasoned (dry) wood produces less than green wood. Burning a few small sticks of hot, dry wood with each charge of larger chunks also helps by providing flames to burn off the smoke.

But let's be practical. Many of us do not have access to the abundant hardwoods that grace the eastern states. Our stoves may not provide complete combustion, even though they are admirable in other ways. And our stovepipe systems may not lend themselves to insulation without considerable modification and cost. So no matter what we do, stack deposits are inevitable. Our focus must necessarily shift from prevention to management.

One way of managing creosote deposits is to remove them before they build up to a dangerous level. In some installations, rapping on the stovepipe with the poker will cause the chips to fall down the pipe into the firebox or cleanout trap. If this is not possible, it may be necessary to remove the pipe for cleaning.

But scraping the inside of a sooty stovepipe is not pleasant work. It is easier to burn the deposits in place. Just as forest managers purposely set their woods on fire at regular intervals to prevent the build-up of dangerous amounts of dead underbrush, it is entirely feasible to set intentional stack fires from time to time.

The people who make Riteway stoves suggest that users set stack fires once a week by placing several sheets of crumpled paper on a hot fire. If this is done on a regular basis, they suggest, there will never be enough carbon chips in the system to cause a dangerously high temperature.

The Riteway people also recommend regular use of chemical soot removers to prevent the build-up of carbon in stovepipes and chimneys. Frankly, I had always been skeptical about the value of these compounds, so I wrote to MEECO Manufacturing Inc. of Seattle, Washington, asking how their Red Devil Soot Remover worked. Their reply was most interesting, and made a believer of me.

The U.S. Bureau of Mines had done considerable research on soot removers, and had found that there was a sound scientific basis for their action. Bureau researchers had also developed test-furnace designs and methods for evaluating soot removers.

MEECO hired Dr. R.W. Moulton, Consulting Chemical Engineer, University of Washington, to do some research directed at improving its line of soot removers. He and his staff built a test furnace and evaluated nearly 150 different combinations of

64

chemicals. They finally settled on a few compounds that were particularly effective without being prohibitively costly, and then set about testing various formulations in the test furnace and in commercial applications. In his report of October 19, 1972, to MEECO, Dr. Moulton gives this description of the operation of the chemicals:

A soot remover is a catalyst. A catalyst is defined as a substance that will speed up a chemical reaction but one which does not take part in the reaction. In other words, by its mere presence alone it very significantly alters the speed of the chemical reaction, sometimes by a factor of a thousand or more times. The mechanism of soot removal is an oxidation-type chemical reaction. When a soot remover is used in heating units one finds that the chemical is vaporized in the combustion zone and then microscopic particles of the chemical are deposited on the colder sooted areas. The presence of these particles causes the soot to undergo an oxidation process and it is converted to a very light gray, loosely adhering ash. This ash normally blows out with the smoke and the soot then is gone; the remaining surface is normally in a very clean condition.

Since receiving this information, I have been using Red Devil regularly. I sprinkle about a teaspoonful onto the hot coals first thing every morning. I notice that when the stove finally stops drawing and I have to take the back off the oven to clean out the passageways, the blockage is caused not by carbon chips (as was formerly the case) but by the ashes of many stack fires.

Fairbanks Fire Marshal James McKenzie says that stack fires account for a large proportion of the house fires caused by wood stoves in Interior Alaska, which is not surprising in view of the rather poor selection of firewood species available in the state. He gives these additional safety suggestions to flesh out Marshal Brunton's list:

1. Use a flue substantially larger than would ordinarily be called for, in order to minimize residue build-up.
2. Prevent small children from playing with the matches used to start the fire.
3. Never leave the firebox door ajar when unattended.
4. Place a strong, large-mesh screen in the flue to prevent animals from nesting. Nests cause many fires.
5. Close all dampers when you are not using the stove to prevent animals from building nests while you are gone.

To this list I would add these safety precautions from my own observation and experience with wood stoves:

1. Make certain that stovepipe sections can't separate accidentally, especially where there is an adjustable elbow or an unusual bend. A single sheet-metal screw at each pipe junction will provide positive protection.

2. Resist the temptation to dry clothes—even gloves or socks—directly over the stove. Sooner or later something will fall onto the stove top, where it can ignite and possibly fall to the floor. I feel so strongly about this that just after drafting this chapter, I removed all the nails and hooks from the rafters above my stove.

3. Make your installation fail-safe; leave nothing to chance and don't count on your own vigilance. If you can't trust a complete stranger with your stove, it's not safe.

4. Provide fencing for the stove if there are toddlers in the household. At least two children in this community carry scars from falling against hot stoves.

5. Never let young children put anything into the firebox, even trash. They may someday put something valuable into the fire, or something dangerous. They may try to open the firebox door when it is very hot, or they may play with the fire and burn themselves or the house. When our two-year-old gets too interested in the stove, I tell him, "No, Son. The stove is Daddy's. It is not a toy."

6. Never let the handle of a cooking pot extend out over the edge of the stove where a small child can reach it and spill hot food on him- or herself.

7. Have a place for the poker where a child can't play with it while it is still hot, and where nobody will step on it.

8. Invest in a good fire extinguisher of a type suitable for wood and household fires.

9. Keep a container of baking soda handy for grease fires; once the fire is out, the meat can be rinsed and put back in the pan.

10. Have a plan for getting water should a fire occur—either a special hose that will always be available, or a barrel of water standing by.

11. Have an understanding among members of the family about what to do in case of fire. In particular, designate a meeting place outside the house where everybody will assemble after fleeing a fire. Too many parents and others have died tragically by running back inside a burning house trying to

find a child who had already escaped through another route but was out of sight in the darkness.

12. Provide rope ladders or other fire escapes for upstairs windows, particularly in bedrooms.

13. Consider having an inexpensive, battery-operated smoke detector to give early warning in case of fire. This device sets off an alarm when it senses a change in the ionization of the air caused by smoke.

14. Remove ashes from the firebox before they interfere with proper stove operation. I remember seeing an airtight heater so full of ashes that the red-hot coals could have rolled right out of the draft hole onto the wooden floor.

15. Don't use explosive liquids anywhere near the stove. In our area this means taking the gasoline lantern and the reservoir of the gasoline stove outdoors for filling. Some people compromise by leaving their pressure appliance fuel outdoors in the cold, and then bringing the can in to fill the lanterns. The fuel is far less volatile when cold, so the danger is reduced.

16. Be particularly careful when starting a first fire, whether at home following an absence, or in an unfamiliar installation. Manya and I worked for a time on a farm in Australia, and had the use of an old farmhouse heated by a wood stove. I made what I thought would be a quick check of the system before lighting the first fire, and ended up spending more than an hour removing an incredible amount of debris from the chimney.

17. Finally, if you live in an isolated area where a fire could leave you outdoors without adequate clothing, store a supply of old garments in an outbuilding where you'll be able to reach them quickly in an emergency. When Manya and I lived farther from the village, we always kept a big sack of warm clothes (including footgear) in our cache as a hedge against the dreaded fire that—fortunately—never happened.

Chapter 10
Getting Wood

When winter settles in and the cold sun traces a shallow arc just above the southern horizon, my spirits rise and fall with the state of my woodpile. When I have lots of wood cut, I feel wealthy. When the woodpile is slim, I feel uneasy and vulnerable. Some people need to keep a wood stove and a supply of firewood on hand only in case of emergency. Around here, wood is all we have. When it's gone, we're out of fuel.

Everybody who really depends on wood probably shares similar feelings from time to time. With other fuels, like oil or gas, a person's relationship to the very basic need of heat can be remarkably abstract, perhaps requiring nothing more than setting a thermostat and writing a monthly check. But one way or another, people who burn wood find themselves more personally involved.

In some areas, commercial woodcutters will deliver firewood by the cord, already cut and split. It is up to the buyer to inspect the wood for size, straightness and degree of seasoning, and to decide whether it is worth the price. Wood is not a uniform fuel, like gas or oil, and no two cords are alike. After a while one may find a trustworthy supplier, and then arranging the winter's supply of fuel will be easy.

Others prefer to cut their own wood. Some fortunate individuals have their own wood lots, and hence an opportunity to be involved not only in the cutting of their firewood but also in its growth and nurture. Often a wood-lot owner has no use for the fuel, and is willing to let somebody else cull unwanted trees and keep the resulting firewood.

Public lands are another excellent source of firewood. National and state forestry agencies and the U.S. Bureau of Land Management all manage some of the acreage under their jurisdiction on a multiple-use basis, and firewood-cutting by the public is often encouraged as a means of removing highly combustible dead wood and incidental debris from logging operations.

Here in Alaska, for example, an individual is allowed to cut as much as 25 cords of dead and downed timber in the national forests each year. No permit is required, but it is still a good idea to check with the nearest Forest Service office. The personnel can often steer you to some especially good cutting.

Bureau of Land Management policy is not much different. Once my neighbor and I checked in at the local BLM office, studied the maps, and then went out to size up some promising locations. We

Figure 10.1—Real wealth. The woodpile.

ended up getting a permit granting exclusive rights to a patch of woods where a new power line crossed a highway, and we cut a winter's worth of wood for both of our families in a couple of days. The only cost, besides our labor, was in gasoline for the saw and for transporting the logs.

And then there are the odd opportunities that always seem to crop up. Once, in Australia, I had access to a huge windrow of eucalyptus that had been removed from a newly developed pasture. Another time I filled the bed of a pickup truck with short pieces of dry 2x4s at a door factory—for $5. Still another truckload of superior wood came from an orchard that was being worked over. People who have an eye out for fuel are always running into situations like these. You might say that, in terms of firewood, the price of energy independence is eternal vigilance.

For cutting wood, most people nowadays favor chain saws, which are undeniably fast and effective. Some models on the market are amazingly light in weight and easy to use; others have extra-long chain bars for oversized wood. Local saw dealers and woodcutters are good sources of information on which models are suitable for the kinds of wood and the cutting conditions in a given area.

A few of us around here are still holding out against the chain-saw revolution, relying instead on bow (Swede) saws and elbow grease. I like bow saws because, above all, they are *quiet*. They use no gasoline or oil, and do not smell; they are light and easy to carry; they have no moving parts to wear out; they're practically indestructible; and they're inexpensive. A good bow saw and a year's-worth of blades cost less than a single replacement chain for a power saw. True, bow saws are slower than chain saws, but that means you spend more time in the forest. They take more work, but when the winter is over they leave you with good, healthy arms.

Bow saws come in a number of standard lengths. After trying several over the years, I've settled on 42 inches for felling trees in the forest and 48 inches for bucking up the logs at home. For a man, I would suggest nothing shorter than 42 inches, and for a woman, nothing less than 36 inches. The shorter models are inefficient for anything but the smallest wood.

Occasionally I've considered looking for another type of saw that might beat the bow saw without going to gasoline power. The search usually leads to the big two-man whipsaws that loggers used before the advent of lightweight power saws. My conclusion is that a whipsaw might be useful for working through a log that is too thick for a bow saw, but otherwise wouldn't pay. A whipsaw blade is substantially thicker than a modern bow-saw blade, so it cuts a wider kerf (groove). It takes extra energy to remove the extra wood. Perhaps this is why loggers called the saws "misery whips."

Whatever saw one uses, it is vital to keep it sharp. A dull bow saw will eventually bind, because the teeth cut a progressively narrower kerf as the blade works its way into the wood. The cutting teeth wear out faster on the forward stroke, so it is sometimes possible to coax a little extra use out of a blade by reversing it in the holder. But eventually it has to be touched up with a file.

A chain saw will continue to cut even when dull, though at the expense of gasoline, time and safety. Various jigs are sold for use in precision-sharpening chain saws at home; they clamp to the chain bar and hold the file at just the right angle. With practice, the job goes very quickly, especially if the chain is not allowed to get really dull in the first place.

71

I'll never forget the first time I cut wood with a professional, freshly returned to Alaska from the big timber in Washington State. His saw fairly melted through the trees, with none of the clouds of smoke, the roaring, and the shoulder-wrenching prying that I had come to think was normal with chain saws. If my friend so much as nicked a pebble, he'd stop, inspect the chain, and touch it up with the file he always carried in his pocket.

Bucking logs into stove-length pieces with any degree of efficiency requires some sort of holder. Trying to do the job on the

How to Sharpen a Bow-saw Blade

Some modern bow-saw blades have teeth which have been induction hardened. Manufacturers claim these blades last from three to ten times longer than conventional blades. Unfortunately, when they go dull they can't be resharpened by ordinary means. (To find out if the teeth are induction hardened, look for the characteristic rainbow iridescence left on the tips of the teeth by the process, or simply take a file and see if the metal of the teeth is harder or softer than the file.)

To sharpen an ordinary bow-saw blade:

1. Inspect the teeth nearest the end of the blade. These will be worn the least, and will show what sharp teeth are supposed to look like.
2. Pass a file across the points of all the teeth, in a continuous stroke from one end of the blade to the other. This is called "jointing," and brings all of the teeth to the same length. Inspect the teeth. They should all have a small flat facet at the tip. If the shorter ones still lack this facet, pass the file over the whole blade once more. Continue in this way until the teeth are all faceted.
3. Now sit facing a window, or go outside, so that good light reflects off these flat spots and also off the faces on the edges of the teeth. Half of the teeth face left and the other half face right, and each tooth has a pair of faces; therefore the sharpening process takes place in four separate passes. Using a 6-inch cant saw file, make the first pass by filing the upper face on the teeth that are facing you (alternate teeth). Make the second pass by filing the other face on the same teeth. Try to file away half of the flat tip of each tooth on the first pass, and catch the other half on the second pass. Take care on the

ground is not only awkward—it's hard work. Chain saws are capable of cutting through more than one log at a time, and there are several ways to build a frame that will hold the logs in position. Long logs can easily be handled in this way if the ends are cut alternately so as to maintain balance in the frame. Likewise, bow-saw users will find that the time it takes to build a proper sawbuck will be repaid well before the first cord of wood is cut.

Next in importance to a good sawbuck is a solid chopping block.

Text continues on page 78

final strokes on each tooth, since these define the final, sharpened shape.

4. Turn the saw end for end and repeat Step 3 for the remaining alternate teeth.

5. Since the cutting teeth are now somewhat shorter than they were, the rakers have to be recessed. File down both tips of each raker at the same time. Continue until the facets so formed are below the tips of the newly sharpened cutting teeth by a distance about equal to the thickness of the blade. Then restore the sharp points of the rakers by filing out the notch between the two tips.

6. Most saw-sharpening jobs require that the teeth be "set" after filing. Setting restores the proper tilt of the teeth, alternately left and right, so that the blade cuts a groove of the proper width. But in my experience, this is unnecessary with bow-saw blades. You can go right to work.

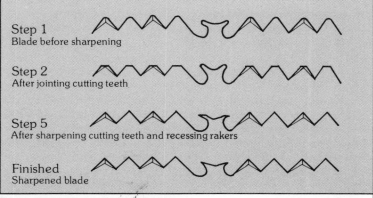

Step 1
Blade before sharpening

Step 2
After jointing cutting teeth

Step 5
After sharpening cutting teeth and recessing rakers

Finished
Sharpened blade

Figure 10.2—Sharpening a bow saw.

How To Make a Sawbuck

There are lots of different ways to make a simple sawbuck. One easy way uses only local materials and a few nails and spikes:

1. Select a log about as long as those you normally end up sawing, and 7 or 8 inches in diameter. Remove the bark. If the log has a curve, be sure to mount it so that the curve is up. This will allow the saw cut to open up, rather than pinch, when the firewood is sawed almost all the way through.

2. Drill two large holes in one end and one hole in the other for the legs. This tripod arrangement makes the sawbuck stand flat on any ground, without rocking.

3. Insert good poles for the legs. Hold each in place with one nail if necessary. Leave the legs log enough to compensate for deepening snow later on, and cross brace them securely.

4. Put three or four pairs of wooden pegs or metal spikes in the upper surface of the log, each pair forming a "V." All of the pegs on respective sides of the log should be parallel and lie in the same plane. The bottoms of the "V"s should be narrow enough to hold the smallest wood that is ordinarily cut, and the tops should be wide enough to accommodate the largest. (An occasional oversized log can be perched on top of the pegs, as long as they are strong enough.)

The one-legged end of the log will be the business end, because it won't rock when you saw. Space two of the pairs of

Figure 10.3—Bow saw and a simple sawbuck in action at spring camp.

pegs close enough together at this end so that they will be able to hold especially short wood.

5. Put a couple of nails into the log to hold the bow saw when not in use. Nail a pocket from an old pair of jeans onto the sawbuck to hold the wedge. Rest the maul and the ax in the crooks of the leg braces. That way the tools can't get lost when it snows.

Figure 10.4—A simple three-legged sawbuck made from a firewood log, some poles, and a few nails and spikes.

Figure 10.5—Another type of sawbuck.

How To Make a Wood Carrier

I don't know how many cords of stove wood I carried into the cabin in the crook of my arm before deciding that there had to be a better way. Finally, I designed a simple carrier that allows me to carry half again as much wood per trip, with less effort (also with greater safety—since my center of gravity is lower, and I can see better where I am going).

A wood carrier is useful in another way too. By keeping track of the number of full carrier-loads of wood that are brought inside, one can estimate how many cords of wood are burned over a period of time. (A cord of wood is an imaginary stack measuring 4 by 4 by 8 feet, or 128 cubic feet.) If L is the length of the carrier and h is the average length of the firewood sticks both expressed in feet, the number of cords carried in n trips is equal to the number of trips x $(L \times L \times h) \div 1600$.

Here are the steps in making my wood carrier:
1. Get a piece of canvas or other sturdy cloth about 13½ inches wide (after hemming). It should be long enough to reach from the floor to the bottom of the breastbone of the person who is going to use it (in my case, 56 inches; I am 6 feet 4 inches tall).
2. Obtain two sticks—1-inch dowel rod or 1x1 lumber—about an inch longer than the hemmed cloth is wide.
3. Get two 15-inch lengths of rope, say 1/4 or 5/16 of an inch in diameter.
4. Drill two holes in each stick, 3 inches either side of the midpoint. They should be just large enough for the rope to pass through.
5. Lay one of the sticks across one end of the cloth and fold the cloth over it far enough so that it can be sewn to enclose the stick fairly snugly. Punch holes in the cloth where it covers the holes in the stick.
6. Tie a jam knot (figure-eight, or overhand knot) in one end of one of the ropes. Pass the other end through one of the holes in the stick and pull up tight.
7. Pass the rope through the matching hole in the cloth.
8. Pass the rope through a 4¾-inch length of ½-inch flex tubing or garden hose.
9. Pass the rope through the other hole in the cloth and then

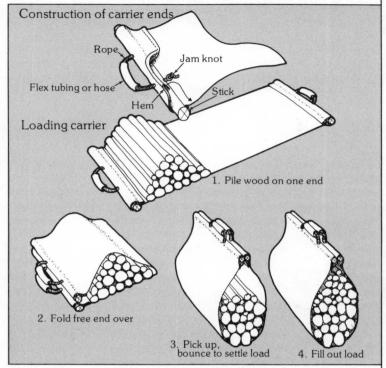

Construction of carrier ends

Rope

Jam knot

Flex tubing or hose

Stick

Hem

Loading carrier

1. Pile wood on one end

2. Fold free end over

3. Pick up, bounce to settle load

4. Fill out load

Figure 10.6—Construction and loading of a wood carrier.

through the other hole in the stick, and tie another jam knot in the end.

10. Turn under a ½-inch hem and sew the cloth together, enclosing the stick.

11. Repeat Steps 5 through 10 to make the other handle, and the carrier is finished.

12. To use the carrier, lay it on the ground, pile wood on one half of the cloth, and then fold the free end over the wood. Grasp both handles and pick up the load. Bounce the wood on the ground once or twice so that it will settle. Tuck a final stick or two into the carrier to finish the load, and carry the firewood into the cabin.

(Part of the force of the ax is wasted if the wood is placed directly on ground that has any amount of natural "spring.") For a chopping block, I prefer a 15-inch section cut from a large log—preferably one that is hard to split, since the ax often cleaves right through the firewood and strikes the block as well. I like to leave the top of the chopping block slightly slanted rather than perfectly level. That way, a square-cut log will still stand on end, while one that is cut on a bias can usually be rotated on the block so that the two slants cancel each other and the firewood chunk stands upright by itself.

Heavy-duty wood users and professional cordwood cutters use mechanical devices to split firewood. (*Wood Stove Know-how*, noted in the bibliography, lists a half-dozen sources of wood-

Figure 10.7—Manya carrying one and a half armloads of firewood in the simple canvas carrier.

splitting machines. The book's publisher also sells plans for building one at home.) Weekend woodcutters usually rely on an ordinary ax. Personally, I find it irritating when an ax gets stuck in the end of the chunk of wood that is supposed to split, as it often does, and I have invested in a splitting maul. The eight-pound head packs a

78

real punch, and the blunt taper makes it practically impossible for the tool to get stuck in the wood.

Some of the white spruce around here grows with a spiral twist and gives us an especially hard time at the chopping block. This leads to a six-point program of steadily escalating countermeasures:

1. Try to avoid the problem in the first place by inspecting the tree before cutting it down. If the bark shows a spiral pattern, go on to another tree. If it is already down:

2. Cut the log into shorter sections than usual. (I've had to go as short as 10 inches, despite the fact that my firebox can take wood more than twice that long.) If even a short section resists splitting:

3. Chop around the edges to pry off the outer flakes first. The core splits more easily once the sapwood has been chopped off. If this doesn't work:

4. Break out the wedge. Pound it into any crack started by the maul. If the wedge just bounces back out of the crack when struck:

5. Set the wood aside until the temperature drops to -30°F or colder. Wood is far easier to split when it is extremely cold, because it gets brittle. If even this doesn't work:

6. Take the wood to a neighbor whose stove has a bigger door, and let him burn it whole.

Chapter 11
The Personality of Wood Stoves

A while back, my neighbor was inspecting a friend's new stove, which was made with one of the popular barrel stove kits and an old 55-gallon drum. He lifted the feed door, looked at the charge of wood smoldering inside, and closed it again. He started to offer a compliment on the workmanship of the stove, not noticing that the owner was quietly backing away.

Suddenly there was a loud thump, and smoke hissed out of every crack in the stove. *PFFFT!* My neighbor jumped halfway out of his shoes, and then realized what had happened: Enough air had slipped into the firebox while the door was open to form an explosive mixture with the smoke. Once the mixture worked its way down to the coals, it ignited. A wry smile on the owner's lips showed that such flashbacks were completely predictable with that particular stove.

Sharing the laugh with me later, my neighbor also told of an old airtight heater he once had. He'd load it with wood for the night, shut it down and crawl into the sack. A few hours later he'd be awakened by a sharp thud, a flash of light and a loud clatter. The lid of the stove would blast open, slap the stovepipe at the far point of its travel and slam shut again. A few minutes later, just as he was falling asleep, the same thing would happen. "Finally," he said, "I learned to weight the lid down with a full kettle. It didn't stop the flashbacks, but at least the room didn't keep filling up with smoke!"

All wood stoves have such idiosyncrasies—in fact, they have their own distinct personalities, kind of like dogs. An airtight heater is as different from a wood range as a poodle is from a Russian wolfhound. It seems to me that small, homemade stoves have the most eccentric personalities, no doubt because they demand so much more involvement than larger or more elaborate commercial models. One of my friends once said that a true stove freak wouldn't like some of the more advanced commercial stoves because "there'd be nothing to do." I imagine that a massive wood furnace—throbbing away down in the cellar, fed a meal of big logs once or twice a day, and perceptible only through the distant hum of blowers and the rush of warm air from a register—would have the least interesting personality. Looking back on various stoves I've been around at one time or another, the stronger personalities naturally stand out the most vividly.

Wood stoves are also very communicative. After using one for a while, a person is bound to develop an ability to know what the fire is doing merely by noticing the little signs that the stove gives. The pop and crackle of burning wood, the accelerating ping of expanding metal, the first musical groans of the teakettle—these are all signs that a new charge of wood is just taking off, and that the stove is heating up. Conversely, a quietness from the firebox, an occasional ping of contracting metal and a gradual diminuendo of the teakettle's song all signal that the fire has reached the charcoal stage and will soon need more wood. In these ways and others, it is altogether possible to know what the fire is doing without even looking at it.

The stovepipe also tells a story. I often check the condition of my fire by looking at the smoke when I'm working outside. In the same way, I read the smoke signals from my neighbors' stovepipes when I go visiting, in order to know what to expect when I knock on the door.

Here are some signs and their messages:

1. Dense, steamy smoke, rising slowly (hence cool), indicates that the stove has just been lit. The folks inside are just getting up and may be neither fully awake nor fully dressed.

2. Dense, steamy smoke rising quickly (hence hot), indicates that new wood is burning briskly, with draft and damper open. The people inside are heating up a cold room, taking a bath, frying meat, heating the oven for baking, or something like that.

3. No smoke and a small amount of quickly rising steam indicate that there is a hot fire inside, but that it has reached the charcoal stage. To verify this, look across the top of the stovepipe at a distant object. Heat waves will distort the image; the hotter the fire, the greater the distortion. Somebody is undoubtedly home, because the draft and the damper are open; but the house is comfortably warm, the stove is not in use for anything in particular, and it has been awhile since anybody tended the fire.

4. No smoke and a small amount of slowly rising steam indicate that the fire is dying down and only a few coals remain. The damper may be either open or closed.

Somebody may be home, in a comfortably warm house, or everybody may have gone out for a while. In any case, the fire hasn't been fed for quite some time.

5. Wisps of dense smoke, slowly rising, indicate that the fire has been banked. The stove is cool and shut down tight. Depending on the time of day, the people are either still sleeping, away on a prolonged errand, or already in bed for the night.

6. No smoke, no steam and no heat waves: There is no fire. A rim of frost around the inside of the top of the pipe indicates that the fire has been out for days. No use in even knocking!

Part Two
Making Wood Stoves

Chapter 12
Techniques versus Attitudes

In Part II we'll explore the world of homemade wood stoves. First we'll go through the construction of one stove in complete detail. After reading this account—which is a mini-book in itself—I think you'll agree that space doesn't permit complete step-by-step instructions for other stoves.

Instead, I'll describe a number of ways to build the various *parts* of homemade stoves. These elements of design can then be combined by the builder to produce a variety of stoves, just as the letters of the alphabet can be combined to form an almost limitless number of words. I believe that if a person has the interest, the materials, the tools and the manual skill to put a stove together, he or she will be able to work from a general sketch of a particular stove and do the designing and dimensioning without further help.

But the first thing I want to talk about is not tools, or materials, or techniques, but *attitudes*. The tendency in a modern industrial society is for the division of labor to be so complete that individuals rely on specialists for almost all of their goods and services. We have come so far from the days of pioneer self-sufficiency that we speak of the "do-it-yourself" movement as if it were some sort of curiosity or fad rather than an expression of man's innate desire for independence.

The trouble is that by depending on specialists—be they plumbers, bakers, or tailors—we rob ourselves of the opportunity to probe the limits of our own abilities. A person who never handles tools cannot know what skill might lie hidden in those magnificent hands. As a result, one who has had no experience with using tools and building things may easily come to consider himself or herself incapable of using tools and building things. Such an attitude—unseen and unrecognized—can cripple a potential artisan as surely as the loss of a hand.

I fell into this trap myself, and might never have gotten out of it had I not settled in the Alaskan bush, where self-sufficiency is still a way of life. My crippling self-image was exposed before I'd been in the valley a month. One day I asked a village craftsman if it was possible to fashion a homemade adapter that would reduce a 6-inch stovepipe down to 5 inches. "Of course it's possible," he answered. "The only question is how to do it."

All of a sudden, I realized that I had been on the verge of giving in to the specialists by ordering an adapter from a far-away hardware store. My friend, by contrast, was already looking through his supply of scrap metal in order to decide which of many possible approaches might be the best. Ever since that time, I've operated on the assumption that if other human beings can do a certain thing, then I can at least give it a try.

Figure 12.1 shows an oil-barrel stove made by elementary school children in a small Eskimo village. Though a seasoned craftsman could suggest a few improvements, there's no doubt that this is a functional stove, capable of heating a trapper's cabin in any weather.

If school kids can build a successful stove, why not you and I? Dig right in, with an attitude of optimistic confidence. If you become discouraged, keep right on going. Remind yourself that you're not trying to build a concert violin or an artificial heart—you're only making a simple container for burning wood.

Figure 12.1—One-third-barrel stove made by Eskimo school children.

Chapter 13

How To Build the Three-Way Oil-Barrel Stove

Ah, the oil barrel! Tens of thousands, perhaps hundreds of thousands of the 55-gallon steel drums have made the trip to Alaska over the years. World War II and the early oil exploration programs resulted in so many abandoned drums that they came to be called "tundra daisies."

But one man's pollution is another man's solution, and the drums have been a genuine boon to people in the bush. Here was a source of cheap, easily worked sheet steel that could be made into such useful things as rain-water catchments, roofing, dog-food cookers, laundry tubs, gutter pipes, sleds, fish smokers, and—above all—wood stoves. Anybody who has traveled much in the Alaskan bush has seen dozens of different designs of

Figure 13.1—"Tundra daisies."

homemade oil-barrel stoves, and indeed one wonders what the villagers would have used for heating had no old oil drums been available.

I was already fascinated with oil-barrel stoves by the time I decided to settle in the bush, but it didn't occur to me that circumstances would quickly force me to make one of my own. As I mentioned in Chapter 1, winter was pressing in when I learned that I couldn't get a commercial stove for my new cabin from Outside suppliers, and consequently had no choice but to go ahead and start cutting steel.

The first problem was to pick a design that would fit my rather pinched circumstances. My cabin was tiny—8 by 11 feet—so the stove had to be compact. It had to be good for both cooking and heating. It had to be made from a single oil drum, with no other metal besides the fastenings. And it had to be simple enough that I could build it under primitive conditions, working on the ground and using nothing but ordinary hand tools—no welding or power equipment. I settled on a little rectangular design, went to work, and was more than a little surprised when I ended up with quite a satisfactory little stove.

Partly out of nostalgia and partly to have a spare tent stove, I recently built another one on the same basic pattern. If you decide that this type of stove meets your needs, I can guarantee that by the time you've finished you'll have a good feeling for oil-barrel steel and what it can do; it really *is* a friendly medium. Should you choose a different design, it might still help to read through these instructions, since you may pick up some ideas and techniques that will be helpful in building your own stove.

The Three-Way Stove is basically a rectangular box with a baffle that forces flames up against the cooking surface. The design is such that the stove can be used with either cooking

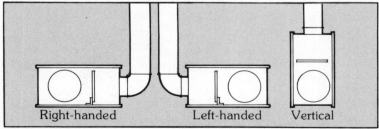

Figure 13.2—Three-Way Stove seen in each of its possible positions. A removable baffle sealer closes off the bottom of the baffle for the horizontal positions.

surface up; a special baffle sealer closes off the opening between the baffle and the stove bottom in either position. The stove can also be used as a heater, in the upright position, by removing the baffle sealer altogether (Figure 13.2).

First, the oil barrel: There are two kinds of 55-gallon drums. The older kind has a round rim and is made of fairly heavy- gauge steel. The newer kind has a square rim and is made of lighter gauge metal. The older, heavier drums make more durable stoves, but the metal is far harder to work. For a first stove, I recommend the square-rimmed variety. Your stove will still be substantial.

Obtain a reasonably sound drum (I always hold out for a leaker—they're cheaper) and assemble your tools. Here is what I used (Figure 13.3):

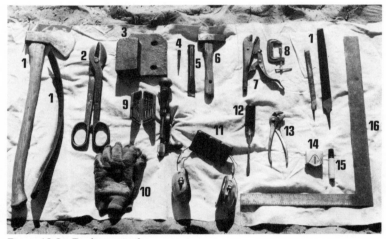

Figure 13.3—Tools required.

1. Cutting tools (old snowmobile spring, file, ax to hammer with)
2. Tin snips
3. Anvil
4. Punch
5. Cold chisel
6. Hammer
7. Vise-grip pliers
8. C clamps
9. Drill and bits
10. Gloves
11. Ear protectors
12. Large screwdriver
13. Slip-joint pliers
14. Steel measuring tape
15. Felt-tipped pen
16. Carpenter's square
17. Hacksaw (not pictured)

88

Note that I include ear protectors on the list. There's no way you can make an oil-barrel stove without an awful lot of pounding, and no way you can do all that pounding without damaging your hearing—unless you wear ear protection of some sort.

I find that the earmuff type is the handiest, because it goes on and comes off so easily. There are several other types that are worn inside the ear. Of these, my favorite is the kind made of sponge rubber. Sponge rubber ear protectors are rolled into tight little cylinders and inserted into the ears, where they expand to form a perfect fit. Next I would choose the swimmer's type of earplug, designed to keep water out of the ears. I have also tried the various sonic-valve shooter's plugs, but I find that they hurt my ears. In a pinch, even a wad of cotton will help quite a bit.

Once you have your drum, flush out any explosive fuels that may remain inside (see following page). Study the perspective drawing (Figure 13.4), the plans (Figure 13.5) and cutting diagram (Figure 13.6), and budget your materials carefully. Make sure you thoroughly understand every step, then proceed as follows:

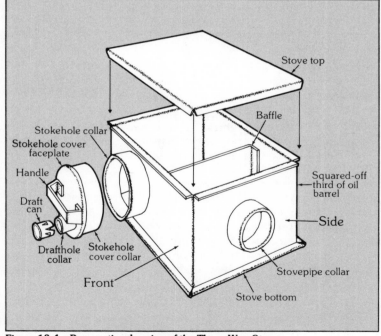

Figure 13.4—Perspective drawing of the Three-Way Stove.

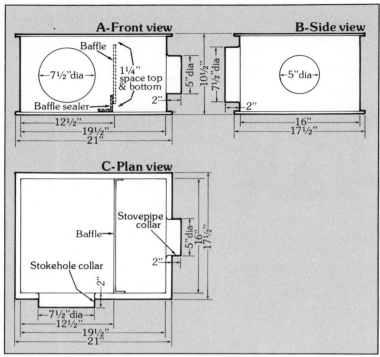

Figure 13.5—Three-Way Stove, front, side and plan views.

1. Draw reference lines. Draw two lines around the circumference of the drum, 4 inches from each rim. These aid in keeping the work square later.

2. Open the drum. Mark a line along the crest of one of the ribs that divide the barrel into thirds, measuring from the rim to keep it even. Cut along this line to divide the barrel into two parts.

How does one cut a barrel? Lacking anything more sophisticated, I made a barrel-opening tool from an old snowmobile spring by filing an edge on one corner (Figure 13.7). With this and an ax I could cut the top off my drum in just under 15 minutes (Figure 13.8). If you have access to an electric handsaw, you can make a faster, cleaner job of it either by using a special metal-cutting blade or by turning an old wood-cutting blade around backwards.

If you have access to an oxyacetylene cutting torch, flush your drum with hot, soapy water, then fill it with more soapy water

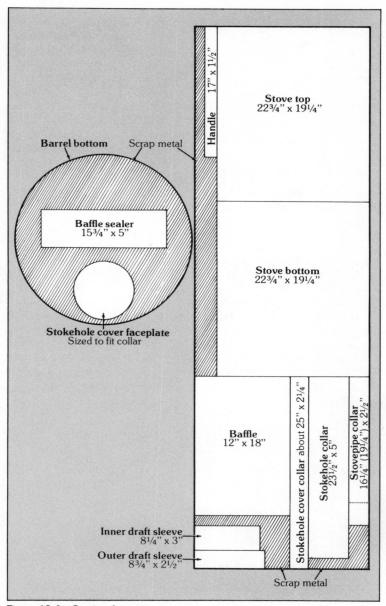

Figure 13.6—Cutting diagram.

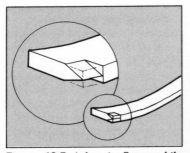

Figure 13.7 (*above*)—Snowmobile spring filed to make barrel-cutting tool.
Figure 13.8 (*right*)—Cutting the drum with homemade tool and ax.

within 1 inch of the top. This will virtually eliminate the danger of explosion. Cut the top off according to Step 3, spill the water out, and cut along the rib as described above.

3. Remove the top and bottom of the drum. Mark and cut around the side of the drum ½ inch below the top and bottom rims. (The rims stay with the top and bottom.)

4. Form the stove body. The one-third barrel will be your stove body. Hammer off the rough edges and file or cut away uneven or jagged projections. Form into a rectangle as shown in Figure 13.9: Mark a line parallel to the barrel seam and 2 inches away from it. This is your first corner. From this line measure clockwise around the drum 36 inches and make a mark. Then measure 36 inches the

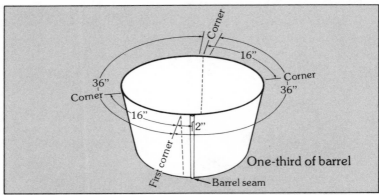

Figure 13.9—Marking the corners of the one-third barrel to form into a rectangle.

92

other way from your first corner and make a second mark. A point centered between these two marks establishes the location of the diagonally opposite corner; draw the line. Measure 16 inches around the drum from one of these corners, and then 16 inches in the same direction from the other to locate the remaining two corners. Draw the lines.

Transfer the four corner lines to the inside of the barrel, and score lightly with the cold chisel. Be very careful not to score too deeply, or the metal may break when you bend it. Now give the barrel a bear hug to begin squaring it up, and finish off by pounding on a squared log or other timber (Figure 13.10). Spare no effort in getting the body as square as you can, especially at the corners.

Figure 13.10—Forming the stove body on a squared log.

What residual roundness you can't get out at this stage will be removed in the next step.

5. Form the body flanges. Fold a ½-inch flange outward at the top and bottom of the stove body. Since your first cuts (Steps 2 and 3) are no doubt a bit wavy, use the reference lines drawn in Step 1 as a guide in marking a fold line that averages ½ inch from the top and bottom edges. Then cut inward along the corner lines from the top and bottom until you just intersect the fold lines.

Now comes a careful operation, in which you form the flanges while simultaneously eliminating any residual roundness from the body. Using the pliers, fold one flange outward along the line. On this first pass, bend only about 15 degrees. The bend will stiffen the side somewhat, but not so much that you can't push the side of the body inward wherever it is still bowed out with the original barrel curve. When you push inward to straighten the side, your flange will buckle, forming a wave. Bend this wave back down while holding the side in. This will lock the metal in the newly straightened position. When you have worked all along the length of the flange and it is as straight as you can get it, make another pass with the pliers, folding another 15 degrees or so. After this pass, you will be able to do more straightening. Continue in this way until you have bent the flange a full 90 degrees, and then treat the other flanges similarly. You'll be amazed at how straight and boxlike the sides have become.

6. Cut out the stove bottom. Now return to the other two-thirds of your barrel and cut it along the seam. This can be done easily with a cold chisel and a hammer (Figure 13.11), working

Figure 13.11—Cutting and scoring oil-barrel steel requires a solid anvil.

from the inside of the drum and pounding against a good, solid anvil of some kind (any heavy slab of metal will do). Measure the length of your stove body, without the flanges, and add 3 inches to determine the length of the bottom. Draw a line this distance from the cut you just made, and parallel to it. Transfer the line to the inside of the barrel (which is still in the round), cut out the sheet, and flatten it by pounding and tromping. This sheet will be the proper length for the stove bottom, but it will have excess material at the sides, giving you a chance to cut off the ragged edges left from the barrel-opening operation.

To determine the width of the bottom, measure the width of the stove body, without the flanges, and add 3 inches. Lay off the appropriate lines on the sheet and cut off the excess. By cutting close to one of the original edges, you should have enough metal at the other to form the stove handle.

The bottom sheet will be 1½ inches larger all around than your stove body. This allows you to fold a ¾-inch flap all the way around the bottom to grasp the ½-inch flange on the stove body, leaving an extra ¼ inch to allow for irregularities in the flange and any curve that may remain in the stove walls.

Now cut notches in the corners of the stove bottom, as shown in Figure 13.12. With the pliers, fold up flanges at a right angle, as if

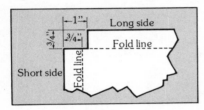

Figure 13.12—Cutting notches at corners of stove bottom.

you were making a cookie sheet with ¾-inch sides. Work slowly; make about six passes to complete each edge.

Repeat this whole process to form the stove top. Set both pieces aside for now. The sheet of metal remaining from the two-thirds barrel will provide almost all of the material you'll need for the rest of the stove components, with the balance coming from one end of the drum.

7. Form the stovepipe collar. There are at least five ways to fasten a collar to a stove body without welding, as shown in Figure 13.13. In every case you form the collar first, since it is far easier to cut a hole to fit an existing collar than it is to make a collar to fit an existing hole. Then you cut a hole in the stove body, somewhat smaller than the collar, and turn up its edge to form a shallow, volcano-like rim. Part of the collar metal grasps the inside of this rim, and part grasps the outside—so that the finished collar can't slip either in or out—or else the collar is riveted to the rim.

For purposes of illustration, I've used three different collar

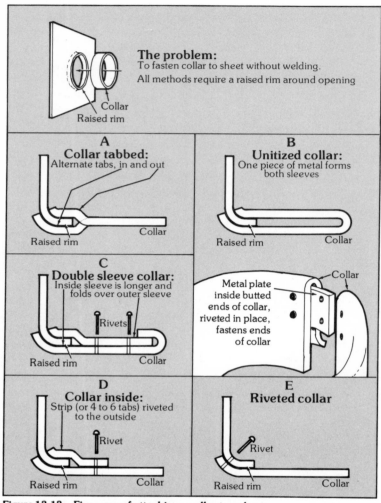

The problem:
To fasten collar to sheet without welding.

All methods require a raised rim around opening

Collar
Raised rim

A
Collar tabbed:
Alternate tabs, in and out

Collar
Raised rim

B
Unitized collar:
One piece of metal forms both sleeves

Raised rim
Collar

C
Double sleeve collar:
Inside sleeve is longer and folds over outer sleeve

Rivets

Raised rim
Collar

Collar

Metal plate inside butted ends of collar, riveted in place, fastens ends of collar

D
Collar inside:
Strip (or 4 to 6 tabs) riveted to the outside

Rivet

Raised rim
Collar

E
Riveted collar

Rivet

Raised rim
Collar

Figure 13.13—Five ways of attaching a collar to a sheet.

systems in this stove. You may wish to follow the directions and gain experience with all three methods, or you may wish to select one method and make all three collars the same way. Whatever method you choose, always form your stovepipe collar so that the crimped end of the pipe fits *inside*.

To build the stovepipe collar by the method shown in Figure

13.13, Drawing A, use a section of 5-inch or 6-inch stovepipe as a form and shape a 2½-inch-wide strip of metal around the crimped end, allowing a ½-inch overlap. For the best fit, arrange the overlap to nest with the seam of the pipe. Mark the strip and rivet twice through the overlap to tie the collar together. A six- or eight-penny nail with most of the shank removed makes a fine rivet.

Center the collar on one of the short sides of the stove body (Figure 13.5, Drawing B). Trace a line on the stove side around the inside of the collar. Before moving anything, make a mark on the circle where the collar seam is, so that you can align the two parts later. Make a second circle 3/16 inch inside the first, and cut out the inner circle of metal. This will leave enough metal to bend up a ¼-inch rim all around.

Bend the edge of the circular hole outward with the pliers to form the little volcano-like rim, sloping upward about 45 degrees. Slip the collar inside the rim with the seam marks lined up and tap the rim against the collar to close any gaps (but don't deform the collar). Now tap the collar down further so that ½ inch sticks inside the rim and mark a line around the collar at the top of the rim. Remove the collar and cut from the near edge to this line to form a series of tabs about ½-inch wide. Fold every other tab outward to match the flare of the rim. Slip the collar inside the rim. Pound the inside tabs down against the inside of the rim, then pound the outside tabs down (Figure 13.14). Keep the collar pressed tightly against the stove body while pounding the tabs over.

Figure 13.14—Stovepipe collar after mounting, inside view.

Although this is the quickest and easiest way to attach a collar to the stove body, it is also the least airtight and the most likely to drip when condensate runs down the pipe. Unless you're pressed for time, I'd suggest one of the other methods shown in Figure 13.13.

8. Form and mount the stokehole collar. Here we'll use the method shown in Figure 13.13, Drawing B. This type of collar is the most airtight, the tidiest, and to my mind, the most elegant of the bunch. Cut a strip of metal 23½ by 5 inches. Draw a line along the length of the strip on the painted side, 2-3/8 inches from one edge. Score lightly and fold over to form a doubled strip. Carefully form this into a circle, leaving the shorter side of the fold out.

(This collar should be as nearly circular as you can possibly make it, since the stokehole cover should be able to fit over the collar in three different positions, depending on which side of the stove is up. You might consider making a circular wooden form 7½ inches in diameter for shaping your collar. If your collar is too far out of round, you'll have to make a second stokehole cover, for use when the stove is in the other horizontal position. Either cover will then work for the vertical position.)

Butt the two ends of the collar together and insert a 2- by 2-inch piece of metal between the two layers to span the junction. Rivet the insert in place, fastening the ends of the collar together. Be sure that the insert lies well up inside the inner and outer sleeves of the collar so that it will not interfere with the lower edges when you fasten them to the stove-body rim.

Lay the collar on the front of the stove, positioned as shown in Figure 13.5, Drawing A, and trace a circle inside the collar on the stove. Cut the hole a bit smaller and form the rim, just as for the stovepipe port (Step 7). Now pry up a slight lip on the shorter, outer sleeve of the collar, using a large screwdriver. Make an index mark across the screwdriver 3/8 inch from the tip as a depth guide for inserting the blade. Taking very small bites, bend a small angle at each pass and work all around the collar evenly (Figure 13.15).

Figure 13.15—Stokehole collar prior to mounting. Note volcano-like rim on stove body.

Slip the collar into the hole and bend the lip of the collar and the rim of the hole until the lip fits nicely against the rim. When satisfied with the fit, pound the longer, inner sleeve of the collar over the inside of the rim, making sure that the collar is pressed firmly into position (Figure 13.16). Then tap the collar lip down against the outside of the rim to complete the seal.

Figure 13.16—Stokehole collar after mounting, inside view. (The gap at the bottom was caused by an error.)

9. Mount the stove bottom. Now fold over further one of the right-angle flanges on the long side of the stove bottom until it is almost flat. Slide the body of the stove into position so that this flap grasps the body flange nearest the stokehole. (The stokehole collar will interfere with the flattening of this one flange, so that is why we prefold it most of the way.) Hammer the other stove-bottom flaps over to clasp the stove-body flanges, working all sides down evenly and gradually. When the flanges are folded over enough to hold

Figure 13.17—Mounting the stove bottom.

the body in position, turn the stove upside down so that you can kneel on the bottom to press it down firmly against the flanges. Pound the flaps over from underneath (Figure 13.17) and finish them off on the anvil.

Your stove body may now have a crazy warp to it, but don't worry—it will come out later, when you install the stove top.

10. Make and install the baffle. Measure the width and depth of your stove at a point 12½ inches from the end opposite the stovepipe port. Cut a piece of metal 12 by 18 inches and fold it, as shown in Figure 13.18. Install in the position indicated in Figure

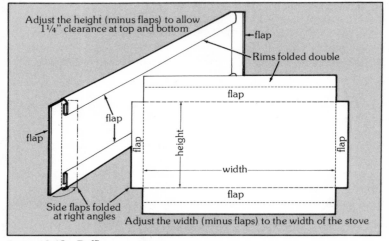

Adjust the height (minus flaps) to allow 1¼" clearance at top and bottom

flap

Rims folded double

flap

flap

flap

flap

height

width

flap

flap

flap

Side flaps folded at right angles

Adjust the width (minus flaps) to the width of the stove

Figure 13.18—Baffle pattern.

13.5, Drawings A and C, leaving 1¼ inches of clearance between the top and bottom of the stove. Rivet four times to the sides. Figure 13.19 shows how the stove should look at this stage.

Figure 13.19—Stove with bottom, baffle and both collars installed.

100

11. Install the stove top. Repeat Step 9.

12. Rivet the stove top and bottom to the body flanges. To prevent the stove sides from buckling and pulling the seams apart under the stresses of repeated heating and cooling, rivet through the top and bottom and the body flanges as shown in Figure 13.20.

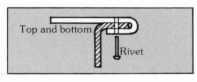

Figure 13.20—Riveting system for stove top and bottom.

Allow 3 rivets for each long side and 2 for each short side, evenly spaced—20 in all. Resist the temptation to omit these rivets; your stove really will cave in without them.

13. Make the stokehole cover collar. (See Figure 13.21). Measure around the outside of the stokehole collar to get the length of the strip you need, allowing ½ inch for overlap. Cut the strip 2¼ inches wide and mold it to the stokehole collar so that it slides on and off with a smooth, gentle friction fit. A collar that is too tight makes it hard to get the cover on and off, and one that is too loose admits too much air for best control of the fire. Rivet it twice through the overlap. Make a mark on both collars so that you can always line them up in the same way. With the stokehole cover collar in place on the stokehole collar, bend a ¼-inch flange

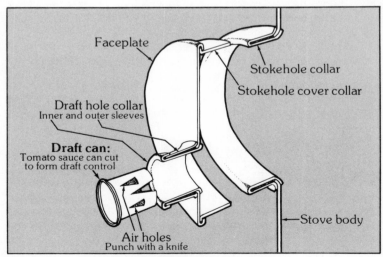

Figure 13.21 —Stokehole cover and draft system.

outward on the cover collar, working slowly so as not to distort it. When finished, hammer the collar as necessary to correct the fit.

14. Make the stokehole cover faceplate. Lay the flanged stokehole cover collar on your oil drum top, with the flanges against the painted side. Trace a circle around the flanges to establish the fold line. Draw another circle ¼ inch outside this line to establish the edge line. Before moving the collar, make marks on it and on the drum top so that you can always align the two pieces the same way. Cut along the edge line, file off rough edges and pound the plate out flat.

15. Form the draft hole collar. The draft system is also shown in Figure 13.21. A tin can, with air holes cut as shown, slides inside a small collar in the stokehole cover faceplate to admit varying amounts of air to the firebox. This collar is constructed according to the method shown in Figure 13.13, Drawing C. First, obtain a soup or tomato sauce can to use as a form in rolling the strips. Carefully measure the circumference of your can and cut a sheet of metal just a shade longer and 3 inches wide. You want the sheet to go all the way around the can and just butt up edge to edge, with a gently snug fit. Mold this sheet to fit around the can, thus forming the inner sleeve of the collar. Now cut another sheet of metal a shade longer than the inner sleeve and ½ inch narrower. Form it around the inner sleeve, with the seams offset 180 degrees. Take care to get both sleeves as round as possible, and check the fit against your can. Clamp the sleeves together so that ¼ inch of the inner sleeve protrudes at each end of the outer sleeve and rivet twice on each side of each seam—eight rivets in all.

Fold the top of the longer, inner sleeve outward over the lip of the shorter, outer sleeve. Then, using the techniques in Step 8, cut the draft hole in the faceplate, 1 inch from the bottom edge, and mount the collar onto it (Figures 13.22 and 13.23).

Figure 13.22 (*left*)—Faceplate and draft-hole collar.
Figure 13.23 (*right*)—Mounting the draft-hole collar.

102

Alternative: A simpler way to form the draft is to cut the stokehole cover faceplate (Step 14) in such a way that the large bung hole of the drum falls where you want the draft hole to be. With the bung in place, your stove is shut down all the way, and with the bung out, the stove is wide open. For intermediate settings, get two tomato paste (not sauce) cans. Flatten the open end of one to make it easier to hold, and slide the closed end into the draft hole; the loose fit gives a low intermediate setting. Cut a ½-inch-square hole in the bottom of the other can, flatten the open end, and stick it into the draft hole for a high intermediate setting. These four positions, combined with the stovepipe damper, will give you the full range of stove control.

16. Cut the draft can. After removing one end and the rim, cut the draft can to the pattern shown in Figure 13.21. Pushing the can all the way into the draft hole collar closes the draft completely; pulling it out various distances gives varying amounts of air to the fire; removing it from the collar completely allows a strong blast of air to rush through the tube onto the coals. A simple handle can be riveted onto the bottom of the can to aid in manipulating it.

17. Mount the stokehole cover faceplate. With the pliers, slowly fold down a flange around the faceplate, following the fold line. When you have completed a right-angle bend, cut shallow grooves into the outside of this flange with a hacksaw at ¼-inch intervals. Cut only about halfway to the bend through the metal. Cutting these kerfs removes enough material that the remaining metal can compress easily as you fold the flange over the rest of the way.

Place the stokehole cover collar from Step 13 onto the faceplate, being certain to line up the marks so that the draft hole will be at the bottom of the faceplate when the completed cover is mounted onto the stokehole collar. Hammer the faceplate flange over, so that it grips the flange on the collar. When finished, slip the whole assembly onto the stokehole collar and pound as necessary to correct the fit.

18. Mount the handle. Cut and mark the handle strip according to Figure 13.24. Drill the holes at each end, then fold along the dashed lines until you have right-angle flanges tapering toward the ends. Starting at the center, pound the flanges over nearly flat—just enough so that the handle is pleasant to the touch. Then fold the handle on the dotted lines to the shape shown. Position the handle on the faceplate high enough to clear the draft system, and rivet twice at both ends through the drilled holes. File any rough edges smooth. Figure 13.25 shows the completed unit.

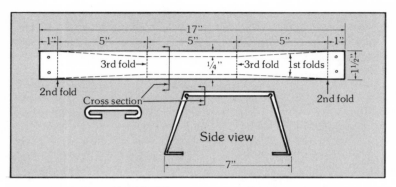

Figure 13.24 (*above*)—How to fold the handle.
Figure 13.25 (*left*)—Stokehole cover and draft system, with handle.

19. Form the baffle sealer. Cut a strip 5 inches wide and ¼ inch shorter than the width of your stove body and fold according to Figure 13.26.

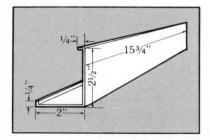

Figure 13.26—Baffle sealer.

20. Paint the stove. If you wish, you can add a coat or two of stove enamel to improve looks and retard rust. Be sure to remove the original barrel paint completely first, since it is not designed for high-temperature use and will flake off after the first few fires, taking your stove enamel with it. Your first fire will drive the volatiles from

104

the enamel, causing an odor, so make sure you have adequate ventilation, or else make your first setup outdoors.

21. Make a trivet. Take the circle you cut from the stove body to form the stokehole, and cut four tabs in it at 90-degree intervals, 1 inch wide and ¾ inch deep. Bend the tabs over at right angles to form legs, adjusting the angle of the bend so that the trivet sits flat on the stove top. The trivet will keep pots up off the cooking surface when they need gentle heat (see Figure 5.1).

Your stove is now complete. Make your first fire a gentle one, both to give the metal a chance to adjust to its new configuration and to complete the cure of the enamel. And make your first fire a time for ceremony. Invite some friends over for the stove warming, and put the kettle on. I think you'll be warmed in two ways—by the heat of the burning wood, and by the satisfaction that always comes when you've made something really nice with your hands.

Figure 13.27—The author and his son light up the Three-Way Stove for the first time. Note how a tin can has been used as an elbow adapter for the stovepipe.

Chapter 14
About Efficiency

Before going into other details of building wood stoves, let's consider the problem of efficiency. Any old metal box with a draft hole and a flue will deliver *some* useful heat, but it takes a certain amount of thought to design a stove that can be called efficient. In the following chapter we'll discuss the various design elements that, in combination, make a stove. Right now we'll consider the relationship between certain of those elements and the efficiency which may be expected from the finished unit.

The concept of efficiency, as applied to wood stoves, is unexpectedly complicated. Any meaningful measurement of the absolute efficiency of a particular stove requires, first, an agreement as to the definition of the term, followed by standardization of the wood used in the test (as to species, moisture content, size, condition), determination of the wood's actual energy content, careful weighing of the wood burned in the course of the experiment, and—most difficult of all—some measurements that would relate the heat actually released by the stove into a standardized enclosure to the amount of wood burned over a period of time.

In spite of all these difficulties, stove manufacturers are not at all shy about praising the "efficiency" of their offerings. Some manufacturers state, for example, that their products deliver "complete combustion" of the wood, basing their claims on the fact that, after a fire, the ash pan contains only powdery ash, not charcoal. Left unsaid is the important fact that a major portion of the energy in the wood is held in the form of volatile substances. Some estimates say that half or more of the energy chemically bound up in a stick of wood can leave the stove unburned, in the smoke. Further, even stoves that deliver reasonably complete combustion may be constructed in such a way that the resulting hot gases rush up the flue without contributing more than a fraction of their heat to the room.

Buyer's Guide to Woodstoves, an excellent booklet published by the Vermont Woodstove Company, defines the efficiency of combustion (Ec) as the percentage of heat released by the wood to the stove. The efficiency of heat transfer (Eh) is the percentage of heat released by the stove to the house. The goal, of course, is to get heat out of the wood and into the house. This overall efficiency (Eo) is the product of Ec x Eh. The booklet continues:

For example, in a good woodstove Ec and Eh might both be 80%. [Figure 14.1, Drawing A]. Then Eo will be 80% x 80% = 64%. This is saying that 64% of the potential heat value of the wood winds up in the house and the other 36% goes up the chimney. This may seem horribly wasteful but it is about comparable to the average oil heat system.

In a poorer stove Ec and Eh might both be 50% [Figure 14.1, Drawing B]. Then Eo will be 50% x 50% = 25%. In this example only 25% of the heat winds up in the house and 75% goes up the chimney, which is a sinful waste.

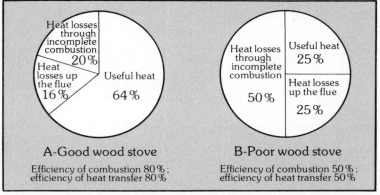

Figure 14.1 —Hypothetical efficiency diagrams of a good and a poor wood stove (from *Buyers Guide to Woodstoves*).

In designing wood stoves it is important to remember that the completeness of combustion will be determined largely by the arrangement of the draft system. Efficiency demands two drafts —one to feed primary air to the coals for maintaining the basic fire, and another to admit secondary air to the region above the coals for the combustion of unburned volatile substances in the smoke. Ideally, both primary and secondary air should be preheated before entering the firebox, and both draft systems should be either independently adjustable or else preproportioned, so that the proper ratio of primary to secondary air can be maintained.

We should also remember that heat-transfer efficiency is increased by forcing the smoke to pass closer to the stove's surface on the way to the flue or by forcing it to take a longer path. Baffles, cooling fins, heat-exchange chambers, convection tubes and forced-air plenums are all worth considering when the stove is being designed. Often a fairly simple structural modification can result in a significant increase in heat-transfer efficiency.

The Jøtul company has published some interesting data on the comparative performance of wood stoves with and without these efficiency-promoting features. In an experiment conducted independently in Canada, two cast-iron stoves were installed in identical camp buildings 1½ miles apart. One of the test units was a conventional box stove with neither baffle nor provision for secondary air (Figure 14.2). Airflow from the draft to the flue is

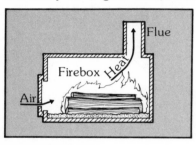

Figure 14.2—Cross-section of a typical unbaffled cast-iron box stove. Airflow from the draft to the flue is direct, and there is no provision for secondary combustion of the smoke.

direct, and smoke may rush up the stovepipe unburned. The other was the Jøtul No. 118. The Jøtul incorporates a horizontal baffle that forces the smoke to travel toward the front of the stove and then through a top-mounted heat-exchange box before reaching the stovepipe (Figure 14.3). It also features a hollow door with a

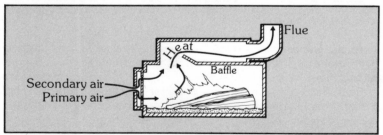

Figure 14.3—Cross-section of the Jøtul No. 118 wood stove, distributed in the U.S. by Kristia Associates. Incoming air is preheated within the hollow door and divided into primary and secondary streams. Wood burns from front to back. Secondary combustion takes place as smoke is entering upper chamber.

single draft control on the outside and two ports on the inner surface. The air is preheated in the door cavity and then passes into the firebox through a primary draft near the coals and a proportionately-sized secondary draft higher up. This design is intended to promote complete combustion of the smoke just as it enters the heat-exchange box.

Throughout the experiment, office clerks in both camp buildings kept careful records of indoor and outdoor temperatures and of the amounts and types of wood used. Although both buildings were maintained at essentially the same temperature and burned about the same proportions of hardwood and softwood, the standard box stove consumed 8.53 cubic feet of wood per day, compared to 4.25 cubic feet per day for the Jøtul No. 118. In other words, the conventional stove required about two cords of wood to produce the useful heat that the baffled stove squeezed out of one cord. And there was another notable difference: The conventional stove was usually dead by 2:00 a.m., so that indoor temperatures often fell into the 20's by morning, while the Jøtul always held enough coals to start dry wood in the morning, and the indoor temperatures on corresponding days never dropped below 40. Anybody with a little training can pick out some unfortunate flaws in the design of this experiment, but on the basis of experience with both baffled and unbaffled stoves, I find these results entirely believable.

The above experiment was comparative only—it measured the *relative* efficiencies of the two stoves. The Jøtul company's engineering department has conducted other tests that shed some light on the interesting problem of *absolute* efficiency. Figure 14.4 shows the results of tests conducted on the same model stove used in the Canadian experiment. Notice that the overall efficiency starts relatively low, rises to a peak of 76 percent, and then declines as the firing rate is progressively increased. I would guess that the efficiency is low at low firing rates because the stove is relatively cool, so that the smoke is below its kindling temperature by the time it reaches the zone of secondary combustion, and leaves the stove unburned. At somewhat higher firing rates, everything works as it should, and the gases are more completely burned. When the stove is opened up still further, airflow through the unit is probably so rapid that the hot gases escape to the flue before they have had time to yield their heat to the metal, so that efficiency once more falls off. At the maximum firing rate, the overall efficiency is a shade under 55 percent.

This experiment demonstrates that the efficiency of a wood stove cannot be expressed as a single number, because it depends

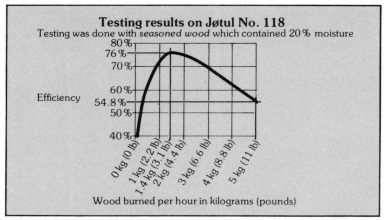

Figure 14.4—Graph illustrating manufacturer's test results on Jøtul No. 118 shows the absolute efficiency. Overall efficiency starts low, rises to a peak of 76 percent and then declines as the firing rate increases.

so much on how the unit is used. In the previous experiment we learned that efficiency also depends heavily on how the stove is built. In the next chapter we'll plunge into stove design. If you are especially interested in efficiency, you might pay particular attention to the sections on drafts, baffles, and heat-transfer systems.

Chapter 15
Elements of Design

The process of design consists largely of making decisions. From a multitude of different possibilities, the designer gradually selects certain elements and rejects others, until at last the final outlines of the object are fixed. In the case of wood-stove design, I break the process down into two parts—the general and the specific. The general phase goes something like this:

FUNCTION. First of all it is necessary to know the purpose of the stove. If it is to be strictly a heater, the possibilities are almost unlimited. But if the stove is to be used for any serious cooking, then its top will have to be at least partially flat, and the firebox will have to be relatively shallow, so that live flames can lick the underside of the cooking surface.

PLACEMENT. It is helpful to know exactly where the stove will sit when completed. This will help determine the general location of such features as the stovepipe port, door, hinges and draft controls.

SHAPE. Will the stove be round or rectangular? Horizontal or vertical? A decision on shape significantly restricts the choice in other categories, and helps to determine the precise locations of the various openings and controls.

MATERIALS. What sort of metal will the stove be made of? Oil barrels can be worked into either round or rectangular stoves with simple hand tools. Sheet steel generally requires welding, and may not lend itself to round shapes without special rolling equipment.

In considering materials, don't overlook the advantages of using ready-made components. It is entirely possible to build a stove from scratch, but pleasing results (and time savings) can also be had by using commercial stove tops, draft sliders, oven and firebox doors, legs and grates—either salvaged from old stoves or purchased new.

So far, we've decided what the stove is going to do, where it is going to be, and what it is going to be made of. Next we have to decide what it is going to be like and how it is going to be put together—in sum, the specifics:

SIZE. This is important. A given stove may be able to heat either a small house or a large one, but the efficiency may be markedly different in the two cases. For example, Figure 15.1 shows the results of another efficiency test run on the Jøtul No. 118 wood stove by company engineers. In this chart, actual heat output in BTU per hour (a BTU or British Thermal Unit is the amount of heat required to raise the temperature of 1 pound of water 1° F) is shown in relation to wood consumption. Naturally, the heat output rises as the firing rate increases. But in Figure 14.4 we saw that this particular stove is most efficient at a firing rate of 3.1 pounds of wood per hour. The chart in Figure 15.1 shows that in order to

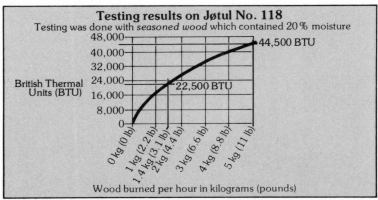

Figure 15.1—Efficiency test run by manufacturer on Jøtul No. 118 shows actual heat output in BTU per hour in relation to wood consumption. In order to double heat output at the most efficient firing rate, the firing rate must be more than tripled.

double the heat put out at that most efficient firing rate, the firing rate must be *more than tripled.* The implication is that, other things being equal, a large stove operating at a moderate setting may heat a given space more efficiently than a small one burning wide open most of the time.

On the other hand, a stove that is too large for its surroundings may operate at such a low setting that the smoke is too cool either to burn off in secondary combustion or to keep the chimney warm enough to prevent condensation. I speak from experience on this, since I designed my present stove to be just the right size for our cabin after the building is enlarged by about half. For now, the stove loafs almost all the time. The wood smolders in the firebox, wasting much of the energy contained in the volatiles, and the stovepipe oven soots up amazingly fast.

112

There are no hard-and-fast rules for sizing stoves, because so much depends on the climate and on the insulation and tightness of the building to be heated, not to mention the efficiency of the stove itself. One approach is to determine the best size for the firebox by comparison with the one in the stove presently heating the house, adjusting up or down according to how the old unit performs. For a new house, one might check out the neighbors' stoves and then adjust for differences in space, insulation and tightness. Either way, it's an educated guess.

If the stove is to be used for cooking, I'd recommend that the stovetop be no more than 9 inches above the ashes. As for length, a longer firebox naturally saves time at the sawbuck, but logs cut to that maximum length may prove hard to split.

SEAMS. In all but the very simplest stoves, the builder will have to fasten various sheets of metal together. Welding and seam-making are practically synonymous, and I will only mention the fact for those with the proper torch that oil-barrel steel can be welded without using welding rod (Figure 15.2). Non-welders have a number of different types of seams to choose from, as illustrated in Figure 15.3.

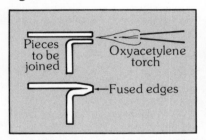

Figure 15.2 (*left*)—Welding oil-barrel steel without using welding rod. The metal parts are clamped together and tacked at intervals to hold them securely. The edges of the plates are then simply fused together.

Figure 15.3 (*below*)—Four types of non-welded seams. Any of these seams can be sealed with asbestos wicking before being pounded closed and riveted.

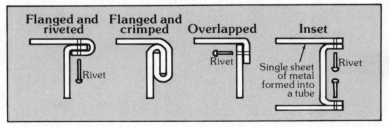

DOORS. A door can make or break a wood stove, since this is a major source of the air leakage which can destroy your control of the unit. Air leakage around a door can be minimized by making the door as small as possible; on the other hand, a larger door increases the range of firewood sizes that can be slipped into the firebox. As a rule of thumb, I recommend that the door be no smaller than 6 inches in either dimension, and no larger than one-half the cross-sectional area of the firebox, measured in the same plane as the door.

Placement of the door involves another trade-off. Raising the door opening lessens the chance of coals falling out onto the floor, but increases the likelihood that smoke will escape into the room when the door is opened. If the door is to be on the stove top rather than on a side, it should be placed close to the edge from which the stove will be fed. This will make it possible to fill the firebox to capacity with a minimum of jiggling.

The simplest kind of door is formed from the piece of metal cut out to make the door opening (Figure 15.4, Drawing A). A good trick is to cut the hinge line first, and then mount the hinges before cutting the other three sides of the door opening; this way there will be no problem in getting the spaces around the door to come out evenly. It is a good idea to install backing strips around the door to seal the cracks and to give the door something solid to close against. The strips can be mounted either on the inside of the stove, on the outside of the door, or both (Figure 15.4, Drawing B). Remember that strips on the inside of the stove will reduce the

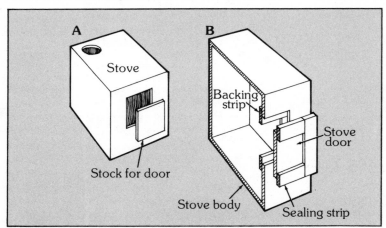

Figure 15.4—Simple cut-out door.

effective size of the door opening, so be sure to allow for them when dimensioning the door.

This type of door is adaptable either to flat or curved stock.

There may be a tendency for the metal to warp, with resulting air leakage, but a good solid latch should press the door against the backing strips with enough force to overcome the problem. In severe cases, a warped door can be unhinged and pounded back into shape.

Another simple door is the overlapping type. For this, a sheet of metal somewhat larger than the door opening is mounted so as to overlap the edges all around. This is an especially handy door for an oven, since an airtight seal isn't as critical there as it would be on the firebox itself. The metal can be stiffened by turning out a lip all around. (See Figures 15.5 and 16.7.)

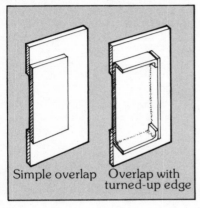

Simple overlap   Overlap with turned-up edge

Figure 15.5—Overlap doors may be either flat or curved.

The cover-and-collar type of door (used on the Three-Way Stove, Chapter 13) is more complicated to build than simple hinged doors, but usually provides a more complete seal. This is especially so on round stoves, since curved doors are harder to seal than flat ones.

Several ways of forming collars are shown in Figure 13.13. The cover collar can be sized to fit either outside or inside the stokehole collar (Figure 15.6, Drawings A and B). I always place mine on the outside, because an inside collar is more likely to leak air, and can be jammed by a firewood stick long enough to extend inside the stokehole collar. On the other hand, an inside-fitting cover can be used with an easily made turned-in stokehole collar to give a flush fit (Figure 15.6, Drawing C).

A box-type door (Figure 15.7) is formed by folding two sheets of metal into a shallow, closed box. The resulting structure is fairly rigid, and hence resists warping. The door opening is cut somewhat smaller than the mating part of the door, so that flaps can be folded

115

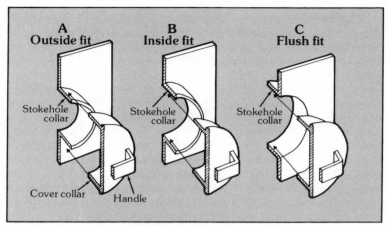

Figure 15.6 (*above*)—Three cover-and-collar door systems.
Figure 15.7 (*below*)—Four types of box door.

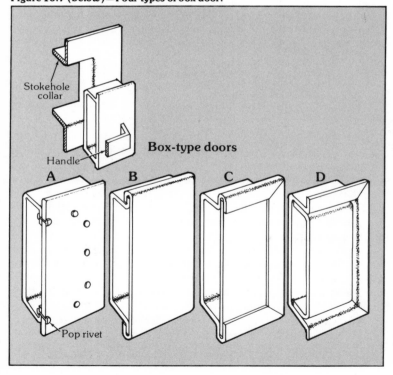

inward and bent one way or another until they grip the door with the desired amount of force. This eliminates the need for a latch.

Like the overlapping door, the box door is especially suitable for use on an oven. The door cavity can even be filled with insulation to help retain heat. The door may be hinged either at one side or along the bottom, or—because of the gripping flaps all around the door opening—it can be left hingeless so that it is entirely removable, as in the cover-and-collar door system. If the door is to be used on the firebox, where it will be subject to intense heat, its lifetime can be increased by placing the draft away from the door opening and by installing a heat shield, like the one in Figure 15.15, on the inner face of the door.

HINGES. The quickest, easiest way to hang a door on a stove is to use ready-made hinges from the hardware store. A few of the many different types on the market are shown in Figure 15.8. Hinges can be attached with stove bolts or rivets, or by welding.

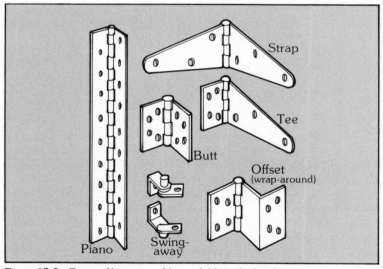

Figure 15.8—Types of hinges readily available in the hardware store.

(For welding, use plain iron hinges, so that there can be no chance that the weld will be fouled by metallic elements in the plating.)

Functional hinges can also be made from scratch, as shown in Figure 15.9. Drawing A shows a simple hinge made of strips of metal folded around some sort of pin. Drawing B shows a pipe-and-pin hinge which requires welding, and is suitable mainly for

117

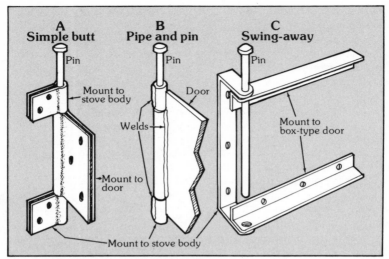

Figure 15.9—Three types of homemade hinges.

heavier stoves. Drawing C shows a kind of swing-away hinge that is especially suitable for box-type doors.

In most applications, hinges are mounted with the pins directly over the crack between the two parts to be joined. For a firebox door on a wood stove, however, it may be advantageous to set the hinge line back from the crack by about ½ inch (Figure 15.10). This way a foil closure pad will seal the entire door opening when the fire

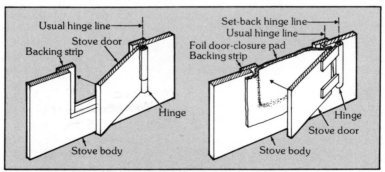

Figure 15.10—Normal and set-back hinge lines.

is banked for the night. Even a leaky door can be sealed very nicely in this way, and the operation of the hinge is not affected at all.

118

LATCHES. Certain ready-made doors and those of the cover-and-collar and box types are self-latching, and require no additional fittings to keep them closed. Others require a latch of some kind. In principle all latches are much the same, but in detail probably no other component of the stove shows so much craftsmanship, individuality and ingenuity.

Some simple types of latches are illustrated in Figure 15.11. Drawings A and B show two easily made latches which require only a few strips of metal and some fastenings. Drawing C shows a more elaborate latch incorporating a ramp. When the handle is twisted, the plate rides up the ramp and forces the door shut. Drawing D shows an internal catch that grasps the stove body. (The hinge pins have to be loose enough to allow the door to be lifted slightly to disengage the catch.) Drawing E shows a latch consisting of a pipe or tube attached to the stove body, and a gripper made out of a bent piece of metal.

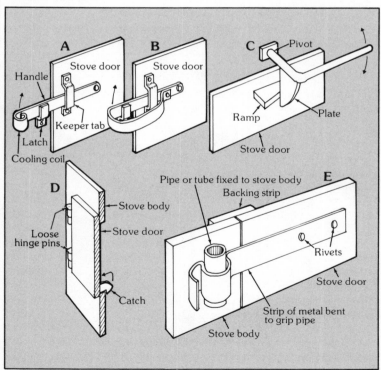

Figure 15.11 — Homemade stove door latches.

STOVEPIPE COLLARS. Please reread the section in Chapter 4 about the desirability of placing the crimped end of the stovepipe down. In making the stovepipe collar, form the strip of metal around the *crimped* end of a joint of pipe of the proper diameter. Once the collar is fastened together and checked for fit, there is no reason why it has to remain round; often a flattened, oval collar will give more usable space on the stove top. Round or oval, trace the outline of the collar on the stove metal as a guide in cutting out the hole. (I urge you not to reverse the order of these steps, because the fit may suffer.)

A stovepipe collar need not be more than 1½ inches high, since this is as far as the crimped end of the stovepipe will go in anyway. It can be welded or brazed to the stove body, or attached according to any of the methods pictured in Figure 13.13. Collars usually protrude from the stove, but occasionally it is desirable to place the collar on the inside—for example, on a stove that is to be used for camping and transported by sled, horse or boat.

Figure 15.12 shows a simple way to form an inside collar. In a very primitive stove it is possible to omit the collar entirely by simply

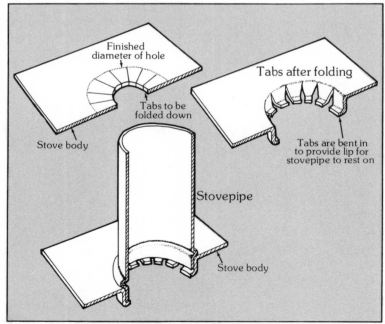

Figure 15.12—How to make an internal stovepipe collar.

placing the stovepipe into a hole in the stove top, but the hole should be cut very carefully in order to avoid the possibility that the pipe will separate and slip down into the firebox.

What diameter stovepipe is best? This depends, among other things, on the purpose of the stove, its size, the dwelling in which it will be placed, the chimney to which it will be connected, and the climate. Six-inch pipe seems to be more or less standard; I have never seen anything larger attached to a homemade stove, although there is no reason why this couldn't be done if it seemed desirable. I have used 5-inch pipe on many uncomplicated stoves, with good results; but if the unit has either an integral or stovepipe oven, I would recommend going an inch larger. Four-inch pipe draws well enough on some small stoves, but the smoke flow may be rapid enough to carry live sparks right out of the pipe and onto the roof.

Should the stovepipe collar be placed on the top of the stove or on a side? A collar on the stove top takes up some room that might otherwise be available for cooking, but offers a compensating advantage: Creosote and carbon chips fall back into the stove, rather than leaking out of an elbow or plugging it up. One way to avoid problems with an elbow in side-mounted stovepipe collars is to fit the stovepipe with a creosote trap, as shown in Figure 15.13.

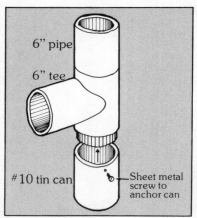

6" pipe

6" tee

#10 tin can

Sheet metal screw to anchor can

Figure 15.13—Creosote trap. Sooty condensate and carbon chips falling down the pipe are caught in the No. 10 can and periodically discarded.

BAFFLES. A simple baffle can improve the performance of many stoves by forcing the smoke and flames into closer contact with the top or sides of the stove before entering the flue. I've added baffles to commercial stoves on occasion (Figure 15.14), and would never build a homemade stove without a baffle.

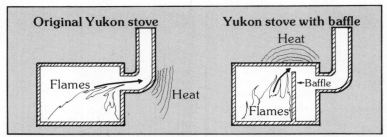

Figure 15.14—Improving the performance of a small Yukon stove by adding a baffle.

A baffle, being a flame concentrator, takes a lot of heat itself, and should always be reinforced in some way. Angle-iron supports, either ready-made or fashioned from the same metal as the stove, can be attached to the surface of the baffle away from the firebox, or the baffle can be made of two-ply metal or of metal heavier than the rest of the stove. At the very least, the working edges of the baffle ought to be folded over double, or even triple (see Figure 13.18).

How much clearance should there be between the top of the baffle and the stove top? This is another one of those trade-offs. If the space is relatively small, the stove top will get hotter and cook better, but will burn out sooner. If it is relatively large, the metal will last longer, but peak cooking temperatures will be lower.

I always decide on a baffle space by first calculating the cross-sectional area of the stovepipe, and then dividing that number by the baffle length. The result represents a spacing that leaves a smokeway over the baffle with the same area as the cross section of the stovepipe. This seems like a reasonable starting point. I may then adjust the spacing up or down, depending on the characteristics of the stove and its intended function.

OVENS. In the next chapters we'll see many different ways of incorporating an integral oven into the design of a wood stove. Remember, though, that it may be better to omit the oven in a very small stove, since the space may be more valuable as part of the firebox. Occasional baking can always be done in a stove-top or stovepipe oven (Chapter 20).

One side of an integral oven usually gets hotter than the other, so that the pans have to be rotated halfway through the baking process. One way to equalize the heat on the two sides of the oven is to mount a heat shield on the hot side, using stove or machine bolts and an extra nut as a spacer (Figure 15.15).

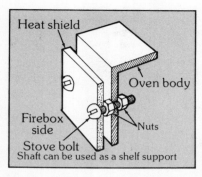

Heat shield

Oven body

Firebox side

Nuts

Stove bolt

Shaft can be used as a shelf support

Figure 15.15—Heat shield for hot side of oven.

Supports for the shelves should be installed before the oven is fixed in position. They should be planned for versatility, so that the oven can hold, for example, two shelves with two loaves of bread each, three shelves with a muffin tin each, or four shelves with a cookie sheet each. Grate-like shelves from some old refrigerators can be cut down to make oven racks, and custom grates can be made from welding rod of appropriate thicknesses.

SMOKE BY-PASSES. In stoves with baffles or integral ovens, the smoke may tend to pour from the stokehole each time the door is opened unless the design provides for a by-pass through which smoke may reach the flue directly. Various types of by-pass systems are shown with particular stoves in Chapters 16 and 17.

CLEANOUTS. Stoves that have special passages to conduct the smoke around baffles or under ovens should also have cleanouts, so that accumulations of carbon chips and ashes can be removed from time to time. If possible, a cleanout should be located where several different interior surfaces can be reached for scraping. Figure 15.16 shows a simple cleanout with metal tabs

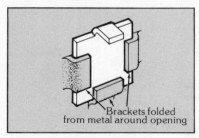

Brackets folded from metal around opening

Figure 15.16—Simple cleanout door.

folded out around the opening to hold a sliding door. A cleanout can also be left open to act as a spoiler when the fire is banked for the night, as described in Chapter 7.

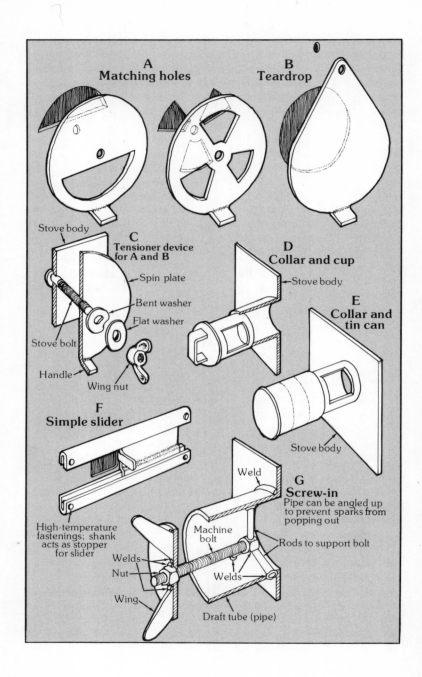

A
Matching holes

B
Teardrop

C
Tensioner device for A and B

Stove body

Spin plate

Bent washer

Flat washer

Stove bolt

Handle

Wing nut

D
Collar and cup

Stove body

E
Collar and tin can

Stove body

F
Simple slider

High-temperature fastenings; shank acts as stopper for slider

G
Screw-in
Pipe can be angled up to prevent sparks from popping out

Weld

Machine bolt

Rods to support bolt

Welds

Nut

Welds

Wing

Draft tube (pipe)

DRAFT SYSTEMS. It is no trouble at all to provide a wood stove with a draft system that will encourage a good hot fire; all that this requires is an opening of some kind near the coals. But *controllability* demands a system that can be shut down tight, and *efficiency* demands one that will encourage complete combustion of the smoke (meaning a double system, as described in Chapter 14).

A common mistake is to make the draft hole too large. A stove properly sized for its environment and connected to a stovepipe with a reasonable draft should only require full draft when the fire is being brought quickly to life. Most of the time the primary draft will be partially or fully closed, so *tight seal is most important.* Several types of draft controls are shown in Figure 15.17.

If the primary draft is located on the door, any leakage it may have can be stopped by a foil closure pad placed over the door opening when the fire is banked for the night. If the draft opening is to be below the door or to one side, it should be placed fairly close to the top of the ash bed, since its function is to maintain a robust bed of coals. In this position it can often be sealed with a layer of ashes from inside the stove.

In the hot-blast type of draft system, the air reaches the fire through a pipe which is either mounted on the outside of the stove or within the firebox (Figure 15.18). The pre-heated air does not

Figure 15.17 (*left*) — Types of draft controls.
Figure 15.18 (*below*) — Hot-blast draft systems.

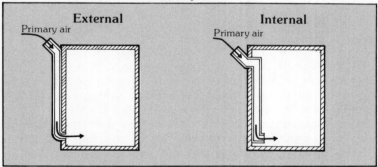

cool the coals or the smoke as much as an unheated stream does, so efficiency of combustion is increased.

Figure 15.19 shows some secondary draft systems. In Drawing A the air pipe runs through the flame zone; the perforations can be concentrated on the main pipe or on the extension across the face

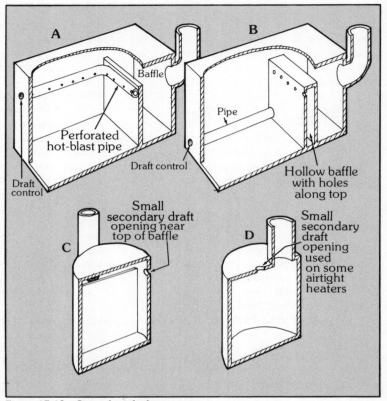

Figure 15.19 — Secondary draft systems.

of the baffle, or else spread evenly along both. In Drawing B the pipe is lower, in the zone of the coals or underneath the ashes. Secondary air passes through the pipe to a hollow baffle, and emerges through holes along the top. Drawing C shows a simpler system, consisting merely of a covered hole near the top of the baffle. Drawing D shows an opening like the ones found on certain airtight heaters. Sometimes you can look through this sort of opening and see the bluish flames that indicate complete combustion is taking place.

Many secondary drafts are located so that the smoke burns off just before entering the flue. One might wonder whether the secondary draft is worth including, since most of the heat drawn from the smoke appears to go right up the chimney. Still, the alternative is to let the heat go up the flue anyway, bound as chemical energy in the unburned smoke. Secondary combustion results in at least a partial transfer of this energy to the room, and the rest will keep the chimney a bit warmer, discouraging creosote formation. The flue gases will also contain far less of the substances that form creosote in the first place.

The secondary draft can also be used to provide "maintenance" air to the fire, with the primary draft shut down tight. Primary air, directed at the coal bed (or even passing through it, in the case of grated stoves), is pretty well stripped of oxygen by the time it reaches the area of secondary combustion above the coals. But if the maintenance air enters through the secondary system, the region above the coals will be richer in oxygen, and combustion will be more complete. Depending on the layout of the stove, the fire may also tend to burn more evenly across the firebox, instead of burning out first in the region nearest the primary draft opening.

Theory aside, many simple stoves will have only one draft system. The opening should be placed somewhere between the coal bed and the top of the flame zone, so that the air can perform both primary and secondary functions. Place the draft in the lower portion of this range to encourage responsiveness, or toward the top to favor controllability.

HOT-AIR SYSTEMS. One shortcoming of a wood-stove heating system is that warm air tends to rise and hang near the ceiling, while cooler air collects near the floor. This thermal stratification can be mild or severe, depending on the climate and the house. Cold air near the floor encourages mildew or even frost in places where circulation is impaired (under beds, behind couches), and is especially annoying if the household includes infants who like to play on the rug.

Many commercial wood stoves have places for electric blowers that circulate warmed air to break up this layering, and the same feature can be included in the designs of many homemade stoves. In addition, there are several ways to get the air to circulate by itself, merely by building some sort of air chamber into or onto the stove. Cool air enters the chamber near the bottom, and heated air rises through outlets near the top.

Several hot-air systems are illustrated in Figure 15.20. Drawing A shows a simple metal enclosure more or less wrapped around the stove. It is open at the front, and additional openings can be provided at the sides and rear. This simple system, while not the most efficient, can easily be added to many existing stoves. My neighbor made one by wrapping oil-barrel metal around his big

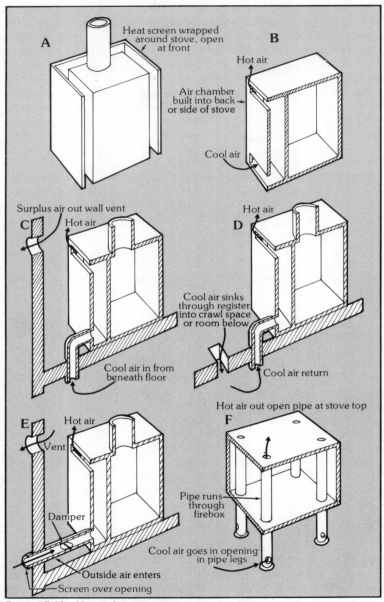

Figure 15.20—Hot-air heating systems.

airtight heater, and gained not only an air circulator but also a fence to guard his toddlers from burns.

Drawing B shows a chamber built into the back of a stove. (It could surround the sides as well.) Cool air enters the chamber through a series of openings at floor level. Drawing C shows the same system with an opening connected by piping to the crawl space beneath the house (or to a basement or room on the next lower level). In this case, the new air brought into the room from below must be balanced by air leaving through vents and through the stove, via the draft. Some say that leakage around doors and windows can be reversed by the use of this type of system; instead of cold air leaking in around a door, for example, warm air leaks out. There would be fewer cold drafts in the room, and it would be more comfortable.

Drawing D shows a similar system. Registers in the floor permit cool air to sink into the crawl space, making room for the rising warm air. The registers will be most effective if placed against outside walls or near doors, where the floor air is likely to be the coolest. This system is practical only if the crawl space is reasonably well sealed against the wind; otherwise, cold air may blow right up through the registers.

Drawing E shows the chamber connected by pipe to an adjacent room, storm shed or garage. The connection could conceivably be made to the great outdoors, in which case the pipe should be screened against insects and provided with a positive-seal damper for days when wind would interfere with proper operation.

There will be times when the hot-air system should be shut off—for example, when the stove is fired up for cooking and the room is already warm enough. The chamber can be fitted with a hinged or removable cap to cover the top, or with movable flaps to cover the inlets.

Drawing F shows a simple hot-air system that can be incorporated into many designs with little additional work. Pipes used as legs extend through the stove at the corners. Air enters openings near the bottoms of the legs and emerges at the top of the stove through the open ends of the pipes.

Another way to increase the heat-transfer efficiency of a wood stove is to attach cooling fins to the sides. I used this system on my current stove, thereby increasing the surface area of the sides by 155%. An air chamber will also be more efficient if partitioned with a series of cooling fins.

HOT-WATER SYSTEMS. Chapter 22 is devoted entirely to wood-stove hot-water systems. All that needs to be said here is that the design process should take into account the need to install either built-in hot-water reservoirs or firebox coils. Stove-top systems can be added at any time.

SHELVES. Many stoves can be fitted with permanent or removable shelves—either at the same level as the stove top (Figures 16.8 and 17.6) or at a higher level, like the warming racks found on some commercial stoves.

LEGS. Most of the homemade wood stoves I've seen don't have legs at all; they rest on various non-combustible supports or else stand directly on the stove pad. But the little oil-barrel stove in Figure 16.17 has legs scrounged from an old wood cookstove, and similar legs can easily be formed from sheet steel.

My own preference is for legs made from pipe screwed into threaded couplings welded to the corners of the stove (Figure 15.21). Floor flanges at the lower end of the pipes provide

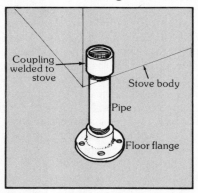

Coupling welded to stove

Stove body

Pipe

Floor flange

Figure 15.21 —A stove leg made from pipe.

nonscratch footings that can be screwed right to the floor. With this system, the pipe can be screwed into or out of the couplings and flanges to level the stove very accurately. Also, the legs can be removed when the stove is transported, or a shorter set can be installed in winter so that the stove will sit closer to the floor and break up the cold-air layer that forms there. I find that 1-inch pipe is entirely adequate for legs 12 inches long, and possibly longer.

FIREBRICK. Many commercial wood stoves feature firebrick lining in the firebox. Since firebrick is a poor conductor of heat, the lining protects the metal from burning out, and also maintains the coals at a high temperature, thus helping to get new wood started and ensuring that the charcoal stays hot enough to burn to powder before going out. Firebrick can also be put into the firebox in the summertime to insulate the sides of the stove and raise a smaller fire close to the stove top, so that one can cook without heating up the house too much.

Stove manufacturers like to claim that the firebrick lining forms a kind of heat sink that continues to give off warmth even after the fire has died down. But if you do some calculating, it turns out that the amount of heat conserved is really not all that large. If I lined the lower half of my firebox with firebrick 2 inches thick and heated it to incipient red heat (1,000° F), the amount of heat held by the bricks would just about equal the amount held by 5 gallons of 200° F water on the stove top.

GRATES. Wood ranges and many circulating heaters are fitted with cast-iron or stainless-steel grates to support the burning wood. Use of a grate permits the introduction of primary air below the coals, where it can do the most good. Curiously enough, I've never seen a homemade stove that employed a grate, probably because a fire on a grate is harder to bank than one which rests on ashes. In our climate, a stove has to be able to hold a fire overnight, and a grate would make that more difficult. Besides, a primary draft placed *near*, rather than under, the coals provides all the air the fire needs anyway.

Nevertheless, other builders with other needs and different ideas may well find use for a grate in their stoves. If you want a grate, it may be worth noting that environmental regulations have forced the shutdown of many foundries in the United States, so that cast-iron parts now commonly come from other countries, such as South Korea. Some of this cast iron is porous and inferior to the old American kind, so it may be better to hold out for a grate salvaged from an old stove than to buy a brand-new part. If you do choose to buy a new one, you should inquire as to the origin and quality of the iron before making a purchase.

ASH PANS AND ASH DOORS. Stoves with grates generally require a pan, or at least an enclosure, below the grate to catch the ashes. The door through which the ashes are removed must be built carefully, since, if you want to bank the fire for the night, leakage at this point admits air at the *worst* possible place: beneath the coals. That's why I prefer to do away with grates, ash pans and ash doors entirely.

FASTENINGS. Stove parts that are not held together by welding or by their own seams have to be secured with stove bolts or rivets. Stove bolts come in either flat- or round-head styles, and in standard sizes from 1/8 to 3/8-inch diameter. For metal light enough to be fabricated into a stove without welding, the 3/16- or 1/4-inch sizes are sufficient. I generally use a lock washer behind the nut for those places that are inaccessible after the stove is completed.

Once you get used to rivets, stove bolts seem gross and inelegant. A well-done riveting job certainly is less conspicuous than the same thing done with stove bolts. But if there is any doubt as to the kind of metal the rivet is made of—or more exactly, the metal's melting point—stove bolts are safer. I remember watching a friend's new stove slowly go to pieces as the rivets melted away and lost their grip, one by one.

In Chapter 13 we saw that a fine rivet can easily be made by cutting off the head of an ordinary nail retaining whatever length of shaft is required.

Pop rivets are also suitable for use on stoves where they will not be subjected to the direct heat of the coals. A pop rivet consists of a malleable head loosely mounted on a shaft (Figure 15.22). The pointed end of the shaft is placed in a special hand-held rivet gun and the other end is placed through the hole; when the lever on the

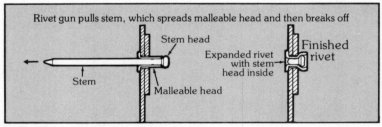

Figure 15.22—Pop rivets.

gun is squeezed, the shaft pulls in, squashes the head, and then breaks off, leaving a neat, washer-like rivet head on the surface toward the gun (Figure 21.9). A pop riveter is fast, and can be used from outside the stove without the need for holding a bucking dolly inside. Again, it is vital to use the right kind of rivet, since many are made of aluminum and simply will not stand up to the high temperatures produced in stoves.

Sheet-metal screws are specially hardened so that they cut a thread in sheet metal without stripping their own threads. They are useful in making lightweight stoves and sheet-steel stovepipe, and also in connecting two or more joints of stovepipe together so that they won't separate.

BUDGET. If you have limited stock available for completion of your project, it pays to make a scale diagram showing the amount of material available and the way it can be cut to yield the needed parts with a minimum of waste. For example, the Three-Way Stove was constructed from a single oil drum, and it would have been most unwise to begin cutting without first preparing a complete cutting diagram, as shown in Figure 13.6.

FLOW CHART. Finally, take time to work out a flow chart showing all of the major phases of the project in sequence. Many operations can be done in interchangeable order, but some will interfere with other steps if done too soon. This is particularly true of welded stoves, where certain internal welds are more easily accomplished if one side or the top or bottom is left till last; but the same thing applies to almost any stove. In the Three-Way Stove, it would have been difficult to mount the stovepipe and stokehole collars after the top and bottom of the stove had been assembled.

Chapter 16
Oil-Barrel Stoves

In Chapter 13 I discussed one possible way of making a stove from a castoff oil barrel, and indicated that there were dozens more. In this chapter we'll take a look at a number of other designs. Any of these stoves can be made from the standard 55-gallon drum or from the smaller 30-gallon type. Remember that the older 55-gallon drums (identifiable by their large, round rims) are made of metal considerably thicker than that of the newer, square-rimmed variety and are a good deal harder to work. Reread the section on page 90 about flushing out explosive fuels, especially if you contemplate doing any cutting with an oxyacetylene torch. It may also be useful to review some of the other techniques discussed in Chapter 13, especially on the use of reference lines (Step 1), opening a drum (Step 2), and forming collars (Steps 7 and 8).

In this chapter and in those to follow, there are photographs or drawings of almost every type of homemade stove discussed. As indicated in Chapter 12, the precise dimensions and details of homemade stoves depend so much on personal taste that I will have to omit them. I trust that the stove builder will fill in the blanks when the time comes.

Many of the oil-barrel stoves illustrated in this chapter feature baffles, for reasons outlined elsewhere. Installation of a baffle may involve removing the end of the drum and then replacing it, so let's go over a few ways of doing this before we begin our discussion of individual stoves.

First of all, decide which end of the drum to cut off—the solid one or the one with the bung openings. For horizontal stoves, the large bung makes a handy opening for the primary draft, especially since it is threaded to accept standard pipe. This suggests removing the solid end. On vertical designs, however, I prefer to have the barrel upside down, so that the solid end becomes the stove top. Consequently, I would remove the end with the bung openings. The seam would be near the floor, which would eliminate any possibility of smoke leakage.

Figure 16.1, Drawing A, shows the simplest way of reattaching the end of the drum. A cut is made so that 2 to 3 inches of metal remain with the end. This metal is pounded and stretched enough to fit over the main part of the drum like a cap, and then fastened in place. This method is suitable for use even when the barrel has been opened with a crude tool, since the metal can be pounded as much as necessary to complete the fit.

Drawing B shows a somewhat neater method, suitable for use when the barrel is opened cleanly with a power saw or, if you have the patience, with a hacksaw blade. First, a backing strip is attached to either section of the drum. The two halves are then rejoined, with the barrel seam lined up, and the second half is fastened to the backing strip with rivets. A small section of the drum makes an ideal backing strip, since it already has the proper curvature.

Either of these methods can also be used to shorten a drum for two-thirds- and one-third-barrel stoves. Figure 16.1, Drawing C, shows another way. The drum is cut just beneath one of the ribs, and cut again right next to the rim. The rib is folded out far enough to accept the bottom of the drum, and then clinched over again. Drawing D shows a somewhat similar method. Here the folded-out rib grasps a flange folded over on the other portion of the stove body.

Drawing E in Figure 16.1 shows a way of making the entire stove top from flattened barrel metal. The drum is cut along the crest of a rib, the metal is folded outward to form a flange, and the new top is installed using a flanged seam. The body can also be cut at some other point than the crest of a rib, and a flange formed by

Figure 16.1 (*below and overleaf*)—How to open and reseal a drum for installation of internal parts.

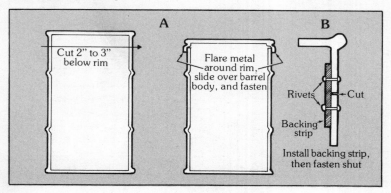

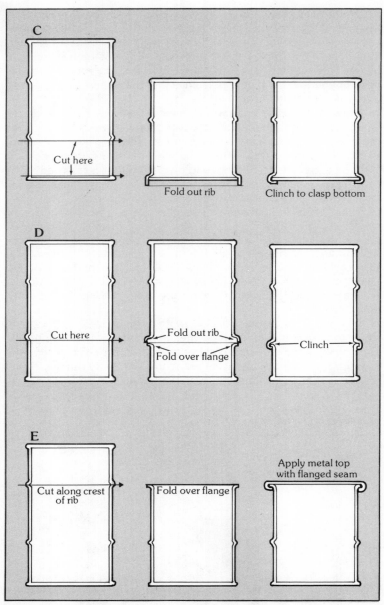

Figure 16.1—(continued)

bending the side of the stove outward. Thus the technique can also be used to replace a burned-out top. This kind of top, being rimless, may be able to accommodate a few more kettles and pots than the original barrel end, since they can stick over the edge a bit.

And now, on to the stoves:

WHOLE-BARREL STOVE, HORIZONTAL. The most elementary oil-barrel stove I ever saw was a drum with a stokehole punched in one end and a stovepipe port cut at the top near the other. The crude horizontal heater needed no legs, since it sat right on the sand floor of a sod hut. I used it for a time, and found that it threw out plenty of heat—though control was definitely a problem.

The next-easiest horizontal whole-barrel stove to build is one made with a commercial kit (Figure 16.2). The same result can be

Figure 16.2—Horizontal whole-barrel stove made with a barrel-stove kit from Fatsco. Note how a No. 10 can fits perfectly over the stovepipe collar at the rear. Made by Howard Kantner.

achieved from scratch by using a homemade door, draft system, legs and stovepipe collar.

Figure 16.3 shows two types of baffles suitable for use in horizontal drum stoves. The handiest material for making them might be the top of another drum of the same size. A baffle shortens the firebox somewhat, making it necessary to cut shorter firewood, but the increased efficiency makes the effort worthwhile.

WHOLE-BARREL STOVE, VERTICAL. An oil barrel placed in an upright position provides just as much stove as a horizontal drum, but takes up a lot less space. The stovepipe collar can be placed either on the top or on the side of the drum, although a top

137

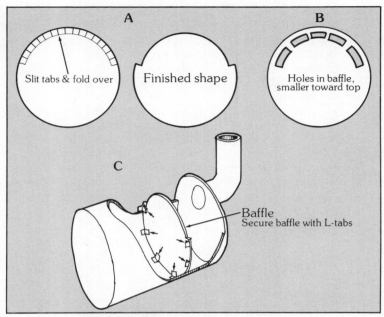

Figure 16.3 — Baffles for horizontal drum stoves.

mount in an unbaffled stove may allow the hot gases to escape up the stovepipe without giving up much heat to the room. In that case, a heat exchanger or stovepipe oven in the pipe will help quite a bit.

Figure 16.4 shows the vertical drum heater in our local church. The elbow is placed well down the side because a heavy cast-iron plate has been mounted inside as a baffle. Drawing A in Figure 16.5 shows a cross-sectional diagram of this stove, and Drawings B through F show other possible baffle arrangements. Figure 16.6 shows a stove that uses the baffle system shown in Drawing B.

TWO-THIRDS-BARREL STOVE, VERTICAL. A wood stove made from a whole barrel may be more appropriate for a shop, church, meeting hall, schoolhouse or barn than for a dwelling. A two-thirds-barrel stove, on the other hand, gets down to family scale and fits nicely into a cabin of moderate size.

Since the drum has to be cut open anyway, when removing a third of it, there is no reason whatever to build this kind of stove without a baffle. Most of the baffling systems shown in Figure 16.5 work in these smaller stoves also.

138

Figure 16.4 (*left*)—Vertical whole-barrel stove. The stovepipe collar is located well down one side of the stove because there is a baffle inside the firebox. Made by Tommy Douglas.

Figure 16.5 (*below*)—Various baffle arrangements for vertical drum stoves.

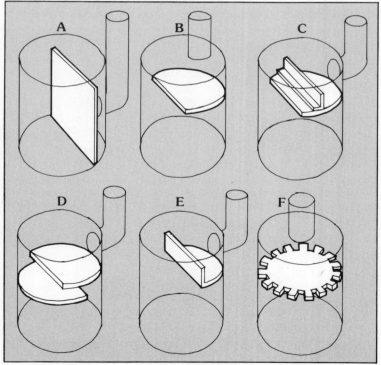

Figure 16.6—Vertical whole-barrel stove with the baffle arrangement shown in Figure 16.5, Drawing B. Made by Truman Cleveland.

TWO-THIRDS-BARREL STOVE, VERTICAL, WITH OVEN.

This type of stove is very popular in our area, and for good reason: It is good for cooking, heating *and* baking. It also gets good marks for efficiency, due to the long smoke path. Two examples are shown in Figures 16.7 and 16.8. Although a good deal different in

Figure 16.7 (*left*)—Vertical two-thirds-barrel stove, with oven. The firebox is in the upper half, the oven below. Made by Isaac Douglas.
Figure 16.8 (*right*)—Another vertical two-thirds-barrel stove, with oven. Made by Oliver Cameron.

detail and construction, both stoves are laid out according to the same basic plan, as illustrated in Figure 16.9. The firebox is in the upper chamber. Smoke passes over the baffle, down around and under the oven, and finally up along the other side of the oven before reaching the stovepipe. The firebox floor and the top of the oven are one and the same; the depth of the ash layer determines how much heat reaches the oven from above.

Constructing this type of stove requires two drums. I am told that in the stove shown in Figure 16.7, the entire baffle and oven

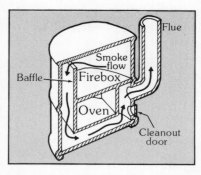

Figure 16.9—Cross section of a two-thirds-barrel stove, with oven.

assembly can be prefabricated and then slipped into the stove from one end. (This may require some tamping with a pole.) In the stove shown in Figure 16.8, the oven is made separately and slipped into the stove from the front.

Since a stove like this has a long and somewhat unnatural smoke path, it should be connected to a stovepipe with a good draft so that smoke won't pour out of the stokehole door every time the fire is fed. I recommend using pipe not less than 6 inches in diameter.

A two-thirds-barrel vertical stove can also be made square, like the Three-Way Stove. This may simplify installation of an oven or some other special feature, but otherwise there seems to be little reason for doing the additional work.

TWO-THIRDS-BARREL STOVE, HORIZONTAL, ROUND. Any of the horizontal whole-barrel stoves described earlier can be shortened to make it fit more easily into a smaller dwelling. Figure 16.10 shows a fireplace built on this principle, offered by Washington Stove Works.

Figure 16.10—The Drummer, a freestanding fireplace by Washington Stove Works. A round two-thirds-barrel stove could be made on the same pattern. The company will sell legs, stovepipe collar and feeder door separately.

141

TWO-THIRDS-BARREL STOVE, HORIZONTAL,
SQUARED. Figure 16.11 shows an entirely different way of forming a stove from two-thirds of a barrel. The body is squared as

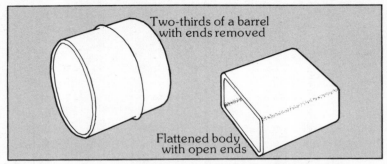

Figure 16.11 — How to form a squared, horizontal two-thirds-barrel stove.

in the Three-Way Stove, but the barrel is rotated so that the openings are at the *ends* rather than at the top and bottom. The end panels are installed using inset seaming (see Figure 15.3).

Figure 16.12 shows an old stove constructed on this principle. In this case, the builder reduced the size of the stove by slitting the two-thirds barrel lengthwise, removing a strip of metal, and

Figure 16.12 — Squared two-thirds-barrel camp stove, with oven. Made by Nelson Griest.

resealing with a flanged seam (visible at the front of the stove top). Figure 16.13 shows a cross-section of this type of stove. Drawing A shows how the baffle confines the fire so that the smokeway under the oven doesn't get plugged with ashes and charcoal. Drawing B

142

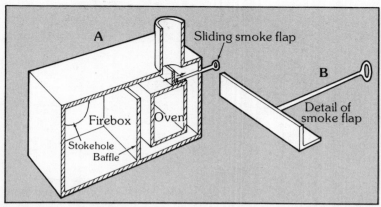

Figure 16.13—Cross-section of one type of squared, horizontal two-thirds-barrel stove.

shows a simple smoke flap that allows the user to proportion the amount of smoke going directly to the flue to the amount traveling around and under the oven.

If the oven is omitted, the baffle can be placed closer to the stovepipe port, giving a larger firebox. The door can also be shifted to the end of the stove, as shown in Figure 16.14. (Note the slanting baffle, designed as a spark trap.)

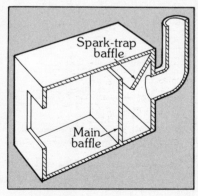

Figure 16.14—Cross-section of another type of squared, horizontal two-thirds-barrel stove.

ONE-THIRD-BARREL STOVE. The Three-Way Stove was made from one-third of a barrel, squared up in such a way that the body was open at top and bottom. Figure 16.15 shows another one-third-barrel stove squared in such a way that the body is more elongated. The stokehole is at the end, and the baffle arrangement

143

Figure 16.15—Squared one-third-barrel stove. Note tin-can damper in pipe, and small area of pipe retaining original galvanized luster just above the damper slit. Made by Oliver Cameron.

is like that shown in Figure 16.14. This little stove is good for cooking and is small enough to take camping.

A somewhat quicker stove can be made by simply leaving the one-third-barrel in the round, as shown in Figure 16.16. If the draft is placed in the stokehole cover and the baffle stops short of the

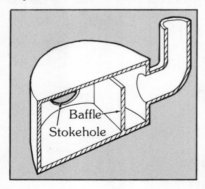

Figure 16.16—Cross-section of a simple round one-third-barrel stove.

bottom, the result will be a Two-Way Stove that can be used with either end up. If there is no need to turn the stove over, the draft can be located around the stove body from the door, opposite the stovepipe port. This gives the longest airflow through the stove. Figure 16.17 shows a one-third-barrel stove fitted with three legs taken from an old wood cookstove.

Figure 16.18 shows yet another type of one-third-barrel stove. Here the builder has formed the body into an oval shape to increase

Figure 16.17 (*left*)—Round one-third-barrel stove, with legs. Made by George Melton.
Figure 16.18 (*right*)—Oval one-third-barrel camp stove (note carrying handle at rear top edge of stove top). Maker unknown.

the length of the firebox. The carrying handle near the rear shows that this is a portable model intended for camping.

A particularly compact one-third-barrel stove is shown in Figure 16.19. Drawing A illustrates how the stove body is cut from the drum; the original curved surfaces are retained, still attached to the bottom of the drum, at front and back. The long sides are fashioned

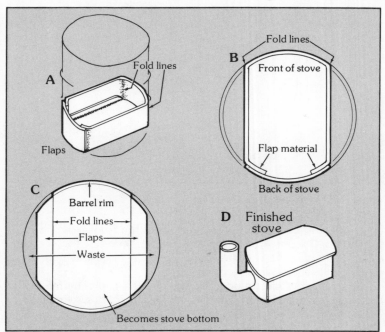

Figure 16.19—A very compact, modified one-third-barrel stove.

145

from straightened barrel metal still attached to *one* of the curved stove surfaces. This eliminates the need to fasten two of the four vertical seams, as shown in Drawing B. Note that since the long sides now follow a straight line instead of the original barrel curvature, they reach the curved end of the stove with enough extra length to form flaps for attachment.

Drawing C shows how the barrel end is cut, leaving flaps that are folded up to seal the joint between the stove bottom and the sides. The basic body is completed by fashioning a top from the other two-thirds of the barrel, and fastening it to a flange formed from the original rib that circles the barrel one-third of the way from the bottom. Such details as the door, baffle and stovepipe collar can be handled in many different ways, depending on the builder's preference.

HALF-CYLINDER STOVES. Another fairly simple stove can be made by splitting a drum in half lengthwise and making the body from one half, the stove top from the other. Figure 16.20 shows such a stove, made from a full-length barrel. Note that the large

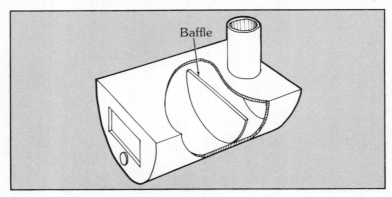

Baffle

Figure 16.20 — Full-length half-cylinder barrel stove.

bung opening can be left at the bottom of the front panel to form the draft. The large, flat top will be hot enough for cooking, especially if a baffle is installed as shown. A large washtub will fit nicely on the stove top on laundry day.

This same design can be used with two-thirds of a barrel, or the barrel can be split in some other way than straight down the middle. Figure 16.21 shows a stove of much fuller cut, made from a 30-gallon drum.

The drum can also be cut to fit a cast-iron stove top, even if the

146

Figure 16.21—Flat-topped horizontal 30-gallon-drum stove. Collection of Pete MacManus.

Figure 16.22—Stove built around a salvaged cast-iron stove top. The old top was shorter than the barrel, so the builder added an oven at the back.

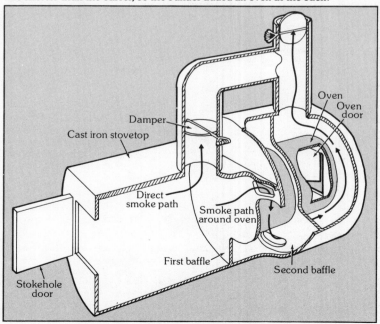

147

top is shorter than the drum. Figure 16.22 shows a stove built around a salvaged stove top that is only about two-thirds as long as the drum itself. In the remaining third of the barrel the builder has installed an oven, separated from the firebox by a perforated baffle. A second baffle, with a hole at the bottom, surrounds the oven. Smoke flow to the oven is controlled by the damper in the pipe which comes out of the cast-iron stove top.

A stove of similar shape is shown in Figure 16.23. Here the builder formed a one-piece stove top and vertical riser out of heavy sheet steel. When the original 30-gallon drum burns out, the stove top can easily be mounted on a fresh one.

Before leaving oil-barrel stoves, we should consider units in which the barrel serves only as a source of steel. Figure 16.24 shows a small tent stove made from welded plates of flattened oil-barrel steel. My impression is that the flattening process produces stresses in the metal which cause it to buckle when it is heated up for welding. My own inclination is to form oil-barrel stoves with as few welded seams as possible, and to save the acetylene for use with proper sheet steel. We'll dig into sheet-metal stoves in the next chapter.

Figure 16.23—Full-cut semi-cylinder whole-barrel stove with steel-plate stove top. Note the double-door stovepipe oven and the inclined hot-blast tube draft. Made by Shorty Schmidt for Jack Hebert.

Figure 16.24—Tent stove with oven, consisting of plates of oil-barrel steel welded together. The lever at the upper left-hand corner of the front panel controls the smoke by-pass that sends smoke either over or under the oven. Made by Don Bucknell.

Chapter 17
Sheet-Metal Stoves

We've just seen that many different kinds of stoves can be built from oil barrels, even though the metal is curved and ribbed and only comes in a few sizes and gauges. By drawing on other sources of sheet steel, the stove designer frees him- or herself to think in entirely new ways and to create stoves that are impractical or impossible to build from oil drums.

But like many another liberty, the freedom from dimension or shape restrictions puts a burden on the builder. By virtue of that very freedom, the designer is forced to make additional decisions, which in turn demand a rationale. That's why I find it so interesting to study homemade sheet-steel stoves. They always express something of the builder's personality and way of thinking.

As an example, consider the little stove in Figure 17.1. In this case, the builder wanted a stove that would be large enough to

Figure 17.1—Lightweight camp stove made of galvanized stovepipe by Oliver Cameron.

cook a meal and heat a small tent in weather well below freezing, and yet light enough to be carried in a simple camping outfit pulled on a small sled by one dog. He took two sections of heavy-gauge galvanized stovepipe, joined them together by their self-locking seams to form a single tube, squared the tube to form the stove

149

body, and then installed end panels made from the same gauge metal (Figure 17.2).

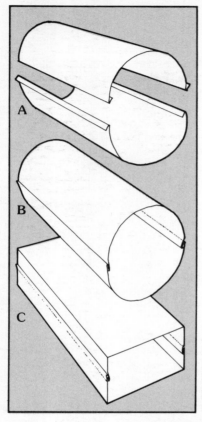

Figure 17.2—Forming Oliver Cameron's stovepipe stove body. Two sections of stovepipe are snapped together to form a single tube and then squared. End panels are installed using inset seams (see Figure 15.3).

Figure 17.3 shows a stove made in a regular sheet-metal shop for the retail trade. The builder used a commercial cast-iron stove top and feeder door (thus side-stepping all the really demanding design decisions and construction steps) and then fabricated the simple, rounded body and the legs from flat stock. The rationale in this case was to turn out a stove with a minimum of labor in a way that would make maximum use of the metal-working equipment and skills available in the shop.

Closer to home, I've already described the tough time I had with a certain cast-iron box stove one winter near Fairbanks. Prodded as much by necessity as by interest—and unable to find a commercial

Figure 17.3 (*left*)—Sheet-steel stove with cast-iron stove top and feeder door. Collection of Pete MacManus.
Figure 17.4 (*right*)—The Ideal Stove. The lever on the left side of the front panel controls the smoke flap. Made by A. J. Klistoff Sr., from a design by the author.

stove that was good for both cooking and heating—I sat down to design my own Ideal Stove.

The result is shown in Figure 17.4. This stove has a unique baffling system (Figure 17.5) that ensures good cooking temperatures and encourages heat-transfer efficiency without shortening the firebox. The smoke flap serves another function besides by-passing the baffling: When I place it in the open position and rap on the stovepipe, the dislodged carbon chips fall onto the flap and slide back into the firebox for disposal.

The Ideal Stove gave us four winters of very good service, and we still use it at spring camp every year. When we built the new cabin, I designed a new stove that is basically the same, except that it is larger and heavier and has cooling fins on the sides and a removable shelf at the back (Figure 17.6). With even less modesty, I dubbed this one the Super Yukon—a name that should be reasonably appropriate once I remove the inefficient draft slider and replace it with primary and secondary drafts.

Figure 17.7 shows the result of another individual's search for an ultimate stove. This one was made by Larry Gay, author of *The Complete Book of Heating with Wood* (excellent reading, by the

151

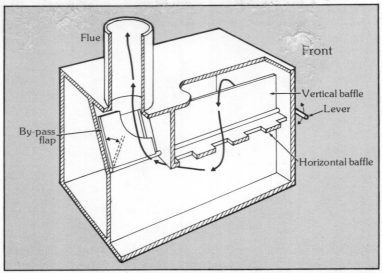

Figure 17.5 (*above*)—Cross-section of the Ideal Stove. Smoke passes over vertical baffle, down through notches in horizontal baffle, toward rear of stove and up through stovepipe collar. When door is opened for refueling, a lever is turned to open flap so that smoke goes directly up the flue.

Figure 17.6 (*left*)—The Super Yukon, featuring the baffling system shown in Figure 17.5. Note also the heavy square stovepipe oven. Made by A. J. Klistoff Sr., from a design by the author.

Figure 17.7 (*below*)—Larry Gay's stove, patterned after the Jøtul No. 118 and now available commercially.

way). The stove is patterned after the famous Jøtul No. 118, except that it is bigger and cheaper and is made of welded steel rather than cast iron. It features a hollow door, which serves as a preheating chamber for the incoming air, and independent controls for primary and secondary drafts. Recognizing that this stove fills a blank spot in the wood-stove market, Mr. Gay has gone into commercial production (see the list of manufacturers in the Appendix).

One trouble with building a really good wood stove is that it lasts too long. A true stove tinkerer always has another design just over the horizon, and often the new stove has to wait until the old one

Figure 17.8—Hypothetical Dual-Fire Range.

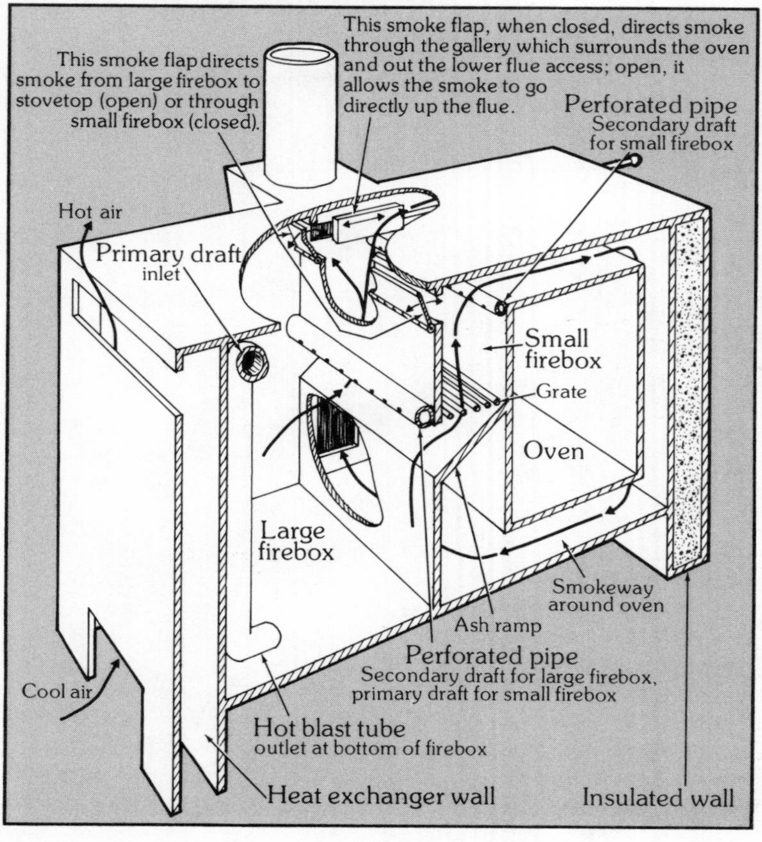

This smoke flap directs smoke from large firebox to stovetop (open) or through small firebox (closed).

This smoke flap, when closed, directs smoke through the gallery which surrounds the oven and out the lower flue access; open, it allows the smoke to go directly up the flue.

Perforated pipe
Secondary draft for small firebox

Hot air

Primary draft inlet

Small firebox

Grate

Oven

Large firebox

Smokeway around oven

Ash ramp

Perforated pipe
Secondary draft for large firebox, primary draft for small firebox

Cool air

Hot blast tube
outlet at bottom of firebox

Heat exchanger wall

Insulated wall

starts showing its age. Figure 17.8 shows the next major stove I hope to build, when old Super Yukon finally gives up the ghost.

This Dual-Fire Range has a welded steel body dimensioned to fit a commercial cast-iron stove top (hopefully salvaged). Its most unusual feature is that it has two fireboxes: a large one for heavy-duty heating, and a smaller one for baking and for summertime use. (It can be *hot* above the Arctic Circle in the summer months.) If the two fires are burning at the same time, the smoke from the lower firebox will be completely consumed in passing through the fire in the upper one. It will be possible to transfer charred wood (with most of the volatiles gone) to the upper firebox with the tongs just before refilling the lower one, and so to have a nearly smokeless fire. Each firebox is fitted with primary and secondary drafts, the secondary draft for the lower firebox doubling as the primary draft for the upper one. A hot-air system draws cool air from floor level.

Sheet steel is such a supremely versatile medium that an almost endless variety of stoves can be fashioned from it. I wish I could offer more examples, but this is not sheet-steel country up here. If you have a design, I'd be glad to hear from you.

Chapter 18
Tin-Can Stoves and Emergency Stoves

TIN-CAN STOVES. Like castoff oil drums, large tin cans may be fashioned into quite acceptable stoves. They are usually free for the asking, extremely light, and so easy to work that a child can make a stove from one.

Take the stove in Figure 18.1 as an example: Seth Kantner was ten years old when he made it. His family depended on the little

Figure 18.1—Seth Kantner, age 10, with the stove he built from a 5-gallon can.

heater when they camped in the Brooks Range one snowy April. Seth's dad told me that the stove was "a little slow at boiling water for coffee," but otherwise worked very well.

Figure 18.2 shows a horizontal stove formed from a square 5-gallon can, with a smaller can in the bung opening for the draft system and an old pot lid in the stove top for the stokehole door. The stovepipe is made of metal from the same kind of can, as described in Chapter 21.

155

Figure 18.2 (*left*)—Simple 5-gallon-can stove. Note the homemade pipe. The draft is in the bung opening. Made by Oliver Cameron.
Figure 18.3 (*right*)—Simple 5-gallon stove that doubles as a smudge to keep bugs away. Collection of Pete MacManus.

In Figure 18.3 we see a little round stove of the most basic form, consisting of firebox, door and flue. The twist latch attached by a bent nail, the leaky door, and the carrying handle at the top suggest that the little unit was built quickly. No doubt it doubled as a smudge to keep the mosquitoes away from people working outside or to keep flies away from the fish on the drying racks.

Figure 18.4 shows a more carefully made version of the same sort of stove. This time the feed door is in the top, and there is a sealable draft located opposite the stovepipe collar. Emptied of ashes and rinsed with river water, the stove doubles as a bucket for carrying odds and ends down to the boat and on to the next camp.

One spring I made a somewhat larger stove from an old military storage can (Figure 18.5). The original can had two ribs on it, like an oil drum. I cut off the upper third of the can at the rib, installed a baffle, sealed the stove by attaching the lid to the rib (just as it had been attached to the original rim), and turned the works upside down so that the airtight bottom of the can became the top of the stove.

This stove heated the tent, kettle and many pots of marrow bones, and kept us comfortable in spite of a constant north wind that shook the tent and kept the pipe ring in perpetual motion up and down the stovepipe. Unfortunately, it disappeared under mysterious circumstances the following summer, so I got another

Figure 18.4 (*left*)—Vertical 5-gallon-can heater. Made by Oliver Cameron.
Figure 18.5 (*right*)—Vertical camp stove made from a 25-gallon storage can.
The baffle is the type shown in Figure 16.5, Drawing A. Made by the author.

can of the same type and made a new stove for our next spring camp.

This time I used the whole can, placed horizontally, and fashioned a flat top that extended back to a stovepipe gallery (Figure 18.6). With this shape, I was able to mount a baffle that didn't shorten the firebox at all, and yet forced the flames to lick the

Figure 18.6—Horizontal stove made from a 25-gallon storage can, with a flat top that extends back to a stove-pipe gallery. Made by the author.

157

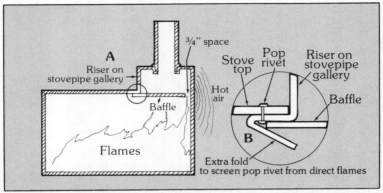

Figure 18.7—Cross-section of the stove in Figure 18.6, showing the horizontal baffle and pop rivets protected from direct contact with the flames by a simple fold of metal.

back of the stove before exiting through the stovepipe (Figure 18.7, Drawing A). The entire stove was fastened with pop rivets; in especially hot locations, they were protected from direct contact with the flames by special flaps of metal (Figure 18.7, Drawing B).

Since this stove was to be carried on the dog sled with the rest of our snow-camping outfit, I made a tapered, nesting stovepipe for it. Using old 5-inch stovepipe sections that were sound except for the seams (which I cut off), I made the first joint 4 inches in diameter at the bottom and 4⅓ inches at the top. The next joint tapered from 4⅓ to 4⅔ inches, and the next from 4⅔ to 5 inches. Two lengths of standard 5-inch pipe completed the setup. (All of the custom-made joints were fashioned according to the method described in Chapter 21.)

When not in use, the three custom joints of stovepipe nested one inside the other, and the set, in turn, fit inside one of the 5-inch lengths. That bundle, plus the other 5-inch length, can be stored inside the firebox, along with a poker fashioned from the handle of an old bucket, a set of legs made from old corrugated iron roofing, a damper made from a piece of tin can metal, and a piece of aluminum foil for setting an overnight fire. Like all of the stoves in this chapter, I like to think of it as a fairly nice example of doing more with less.

EMERGENCY STOVES. The word "emergency" may be too strong. I mean to describe a few stoves that people put together on the spur of the moment, from whatever materials were at hand. Perhaps they had been stranded without a stove under weather conditions that made some sort of heating system necessary, or maybe they had just decided to brew up a quick mug of tea.

One blustery day, just before freezeup, Manya and I were kayaking downriver to our *ukiuvik* (wintering place), when we came upon an Eskimo hunting camp. More than ready for a warmup, we accepted the invitation waved from shore, nosed the kayak in beside the other boats, and went up to the small tent. Smoke was billowing out of its open flaps, and the kettle was heating on the simplest stove I'd ever seen.

One of the hunters had taken an empty 5-gallon can and simply cut two holes in it with his knife: a large one in one side (the stove top) that was just a shade smaller than the kettle, and a small one in the upper part of one end to serve as a smoke exit (Figure 18.8). The bung opening, in the lower part of the other end, served as the draft hole. To load the stove, his wife simply lifted the kettle, stuffed dry grass into the "firebox," and put the kettle back in place.

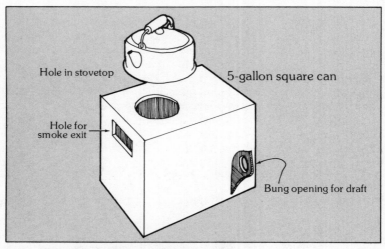

Figure 18.8—The simplest stove I've ever seen.

Then there was the time the local pilot flew over to the hot springs, neglecting to take a stove. In spite of the warm water and the almost continual spring daylight, evenings in the tent were uncomfortably cool. So he cut a door opening in one end of a 5-gallon can and attached a stovepipe made from a series of tin cans, one on top of another (Figure 18.9). Simple as it was, the little stove took the chill off the tent very nicely, making it much easier to leave the springs after a good soak.

159

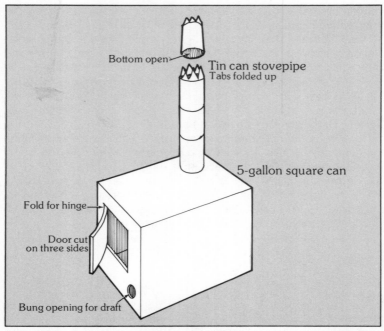

Figure 18.9—A tin-can emergency stove with a tin-can pipe. Designed by Dan
Denslow and Tommy Lee.

Another stove, that Manya noticed in the village, speaks of an
ocean storm that pinned a family down in a hasty camp on the
Arctic Coast. Faced with the prospect of several days of discomfort,
the craftsman sacrificed one of his 6-gallon portable outboard fuel
tanks in order to make a tent heater that would make use of the

Figure 18.10—Camp stove made
from an outboard fuel tank. The
handle came off the tank, and the
stoke-hole cover was once the
reservoir of a gasoline lantern. Made
by Nelson Griest.

160

tangled skeins of driftwood lining the beach (Figure 18.10). The stokehole has a proper collar, cover and draft system, and the far end is fitted with a stovepipe collar. Because of its durability and handy flat cooking top, this little stove outlived the emergency and became a prized all-around boating stove.

Chapter 19
Coking Stoves

A coking or downdraft stove is one in which the smoke must pass through the coals before reaching the flue. The high temperature of the coal bed encourages complete combustion, thus making available the 50 percent or so of the wood's energy that can (and often does) pass out through the chimney in the form of smoke. New fuel is first coked (distilled), and then gradually settles down into the zone of active combustion to provide heat for the next charge. Properly operating, such a stove should be smokeless and free of creosote.

The main challenge in building a coking stove is to get the smoke to go *downward* rather than upward. Larry Gay, in *The Complete Book of Heating with Wood,* gives an interesting account of how Benjamin Franklin conceived, designed and successfully operated a downdraft stove. Franklin stressed the necessity of connecting his creation to a chimney with a strong draft, and the same requirement holds for any downdraft stove we might build. Today, a builder may be able to compensate for insufficient draft by installing a small booster fan in the stovepipe.

A downdraft stove consists of an inner wood magazine (or coking oven) where the wood is distilled, and an outer box through which the flames and hot gases travel on the way to the flue. Complete combustion occurs near the junction of the inner and outer chambers, and it is here that secondary air should be introduced. When the unit is operating in the downdraft mode, primary air enters the coking oven and travels down toward the coal bed, carrying the smoke and distillation products with it. As this mixture passes through the coals, the oxygen is consumed in maintaining the fire, while the volatiles are either burned, broken down into simpler compounds, or simply heated. Any flammable substances that manage to leave the coal bed are immediately consumed in the secondary combustion process, providing heat to continue the wood volatilization and to warm the room.

Larry Gay writes that "true downdraft stoves and furnaces have appeared on the American market from time to time, but none has survived because of the same difficulties that Franklin experienced"—chiefly inadequate draft, which allowed smoke to puff into the room when the feed door was opened. Perhaps the reason these units failed the test of the marketplace is that too few people were willing to maintain a stove that required understanding, skill and determination to operate. In our present era of fuel shortages, however, we may expect renewed interest in efficiency and economy, and downdraft stoves may find increasing favor. Very likely much of the developmental work will have to be done by amateur stove builders.

The only information I have been able to find on homemade

Figure 19.1—Ted Ledger's two-barrel coking stove. For proper operation, all seams and the ash and feed doors must be airtight, so that the fire can get air only through the primary draft. The sand on top of the stove seals the feed door (the fit should be checked each time the fire is stoked).

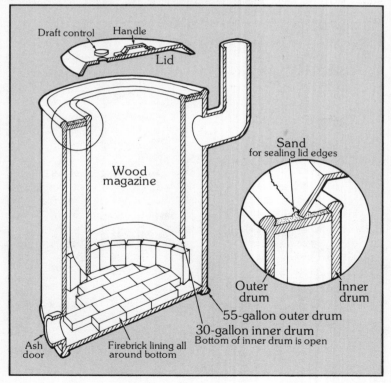

coking stoves is one article in the May, 1974 issue of *Alternative Sources of Energy*. The author, Ted Ledger, gives a simple design for constructing a downdraft stove from two drums, one inside the other (Figure 19.1). Like all downdraft stoves, it operates in the updraft mode at first, with primary air admitted through the ash door. When the coal bed is established and the stove and flue are warm enough to provide adequate draft, the ash door is closed and the unit switches over to the downdraft mode.

Mr. Ledger has been kind enough to provide me with a description of another coking stove, which he built a number of years ago. He had seen a drawing of a commercial stove in a Swedish technical publication some years previously, and built his own version from memory (Figure 19.2). The heater, as it turned out, was so powerful that it was not suitable for use in the small cabin for which it was built.

Figure 19.2—Another type of coking stove by Ted Ledger. The triangular stiffener doubles as a heat exchanger.

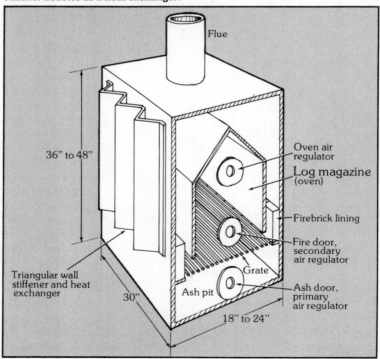

This brings up another characteristic of downdraft stoves. Complete combustion means live flames, and live flames mean fairly high temperatures. A stove that is getting nearly *all* the energy out of the wood is going to be a potent heater. It stands to reason that such a stove should be somewhat smaller than a less efficient unit.

My inclination would be to try a stove with a tall coking chamber and a small active flame zone, as shown in Figure 19.3. In this design, the coking chamber is open only at the front edge, facing

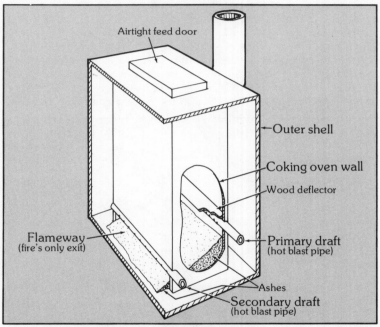

Figure 19.3—Author's hypothetical coking stove designed with a tall coking chamber and a small active flame zone.

the ash door. The accumulated ashes in the fuel magazine will naturally slope toward this opening, and consequently the coals will always tend to roll down to the place where they will do the most good. The size of the flameway is adjustable, merely by varying the quantity of ashes left in the bottom of the stove. Note that the primary air enters through a control on the side, so that the air travels more sideways than downward. Secondary air enters through a hot-blast perforated pipe along the upper edge of the flameway, where it will no doubt perform some primary draft function as well, keeping the charcoal bed glowing.

While we're thinking about complete combustion, we should perhaps consider other ways of burning the smoke besides forcing it to go down through the coals. Larry Gay mentions another Benjamin Franklin invention—the rotary grate. After wood was added, this grate was closed and turned over, so that the coals rested on top of the fresh wood. The smoke rose upward and passed through the coals, where it was completely consumed. On a much smaller scale, it is possible in some stoves to shove the coals to one side of the firebox, lay a stick of new wood on the ashes, and cover it over again with the active coals. Try it once for a very convincing demonstration of smokeless, complete combustion.

Another approach to the coking problem is to have an entirely separate coking compartment for the new wood, connected by pipe to the main firebox (Figure 19.4). The idea is that the heat of the main fire will distill the wood in the coking chamber, and that

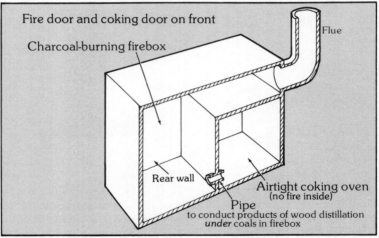

Figure 19.4—Hypothetical charcoal-burning, smokeless, complete combustion updraft stove with separate firebox and coking oven.

the combustible distillation products will enter the firebox *underneath* the coals. The stove always operates in the standard updraft fashion, whether or not the coking feature is in use.

Unfortunately, the wood must be handled twice—once to stoke the coking chamber, and again to transfer the devolatilized fuel to the main firebox. But this could be accomplished fairly easily with a pair of sturdy tongs, especially if the feed doors were placed close together. The extra effort would be paid for in increased efficiency and fuel savings.

With this brief description of coking stoves, I turn it over to you. If you are thinking of building one, know that you are in the vanguard of wood-stove research. If you have already built one, I'd certainly be interested in knowing what it's like and how it has worked for you.

Chapter 20
Stove-Top and Stovepipe Ovens

STOVE-TOP OVENS. When Manya and I first set up housekeeping, our "house" was a 7- by 9-foot wall tent on the bank of a river. During that summer we slowly accumulated materials from the forest for building our cabin. In August, when the blueberries ripened, we'd spend some time every day up on the tundra gathering the fruit, and then bake something special when we got back to camp.

Our outfit was pretty slim, so Manya's first stove-top oven was nothing more than a 5-gallon kerosene can with one side cut out (Figure 20.1). She'd set the baking pan on a metal stand or "lifter"

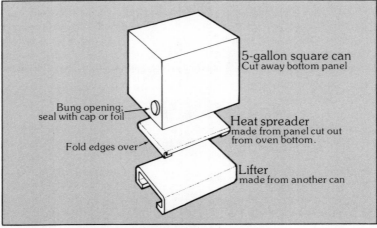

Figure 20.1—A simple tin-can stove-top oven.

(made of metal from another can) in order to get it up into the hottest air and also to keep the bottom from burning. I also made a heat spreader out of the panel cut from the side of the can that became the oven. The spreader went on top of the lifter when

Manya used the oven on the wood stove, and underneath the lifter when she used it on the gasoline camp stove.

The next-generation stove-top oven was built on the same pattern, except that it consisted of two cans—one inside the other (Figure 20.2). The outer can is just the same as the can in the original design, except that a little extra metal remains around the

Figure 20.2—Oat crunch toasting under an insulated double-walled 5-gallon-can stove-top oven. Designed by Dan Denslow and made by the author.

opening to form retaining flaps for the lining. The inner can is cut across all four upper corners and pinched along the edges in order to make it small enough to slide inside the outer can. It is then covered with a layer of fiberglass or asbestos insulation, slipped in place, and secured with the retaining flaps of the outer can. The resulting oven has a shade less capacity than the single-can model, but it bakes more quickly and more evenly due to the insulation (Figure 20.3).

A third-generation stove-top oven undoubtedly would have been made of light-gauge sheet metal, with insulated walls and perhaps a door and shelves. But I never got that far—I was sidetracked by stovepipe ovens.

STOVEPIPE OVENS. The great advantage of a stovepipe oven is that one can be added to almost any existing stove; the only requirement is that there be enough physical space (clearance from the wall, and vertical distance between the stovepipe collar and the chimney inlet or ceiling). It is tempting to add that a stovepipe oven operates entirely on waste heat, but this may not be the case. We

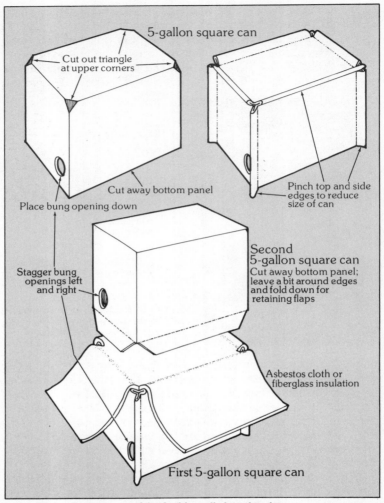

5-gallon square can

Cut out triangle at upper corners

Cut away bottom panel

Place bung opening down

Pinch top and side edges to reduce size of can

Stagger bung openings left and right

Second 5-gallon square can
Cut away bottom panel; leave a bit around edges and fold down for retaining flaps

Asbestos cloth or fiberglass insulation

First 5-gallon square can

Figure 20.3—Construction of the double-walled insulated tin-can stove-top oven.

find it necessary to build a special baking fire that sends much more heat up the stovepipe than we would otherwise tolerate.

Most stovepipe ovens are similar in construction to the one shown in Figure 20.4. The round oven chamber is encased in a larger round shell, with a smokeway between the walls. The back of the oven chamber may touch the back of the outer shell, or there

Figure 20.4—Typical stovepipe oven. Note that the shelf can be turned upside down if the oven should be inverted in the next installation. Collection of Pete MacManus.

may be a space between them for the passage of smoke. For versatility, the shelving is made in such a way that the oven can be used with either end up.

Figure 16.23 shows a homemade unit that differs from most in having a door at either end. When both doors are open, the oven functions as an efficient heat exchanger.

The raw materials for making a simple round stovepipe oven of this type are two cans of appropriate sizes, and metal for making the door, hinge, latch, shelving and collars. Most of the critical dimensions will be determined by the sizes of the cans. The most important measurement is the annular space (smokeway) between the walls. If the space is too big, the oven may not heat well; if it is too small, the smokeway may soot up quickly, impairing the draft and creating the possibility of stack fires. (I notice that the Louisville Tin & Stove Company unit uses a 1½-inch annular spacing. This gives a smokeway with an area about one and a half times the cross-sectional area of the stovepipe—a useful rule of thumb.)

I have never been able to locate two cans of the right relative diameters to make a round stovepipe oven, so I designed one requiring only flat stock (see Figure 17.6). In this unit the incoming smoke is deflected by a flame spreader and then passes around and behind the oven chamber.

I made two critical mistakes in designing this oven, and both of them relate to the creosote problem. First, the annular space of 1 inch that I allowed is simply too small, and poor draft is a chronic

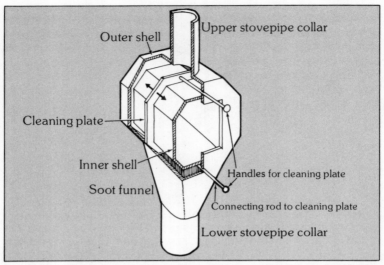

Figure 20.5—Welded plate octagonal stovepipe oven. This shape should solve the problem of accumulation of carbon chips on flat-plate surfaces.

problem. Secondly, dislodged carbon chips collect on the flat surfaces, blocking the draft even further. Eventually, the draft is so weak that it isn't even possible to get the oven hot enough to start a stack fire to burn off the clogging debris, and then the back of the oven has to be removed and all the accumulated junk laboriously scraped out—a 45-minute job.

Still, I like the idea of a welded, flat-plate stovepipe oven, because heavy steel lasts longer and heats more evenly than tin cans do. Next time I'll make the unit in an octagonal shape, with the lower portion designed in such a way that stovepipe debris can funnel back down into the stove (Figure 20.5). There will also be an internal cleaning device that will eliminate the need for a removable back (with its potential for dripping creosote) and manual scraping. Believe me, scraping soot from a stovepipe oven gets tiresome after the first few times.

Chapter 21

Making Stovepipe, Dampers and Adapters

Commercial stovepipe is durable, dependable, uniform and reasonably inexpensive. Considering the disastrous consequences that could follow a stovepipe failure, I have always favored using the ready-made variety. But there are situations where it is desirable or necessary to make stovepipe, and there are several ways of doing so. The main points to remember are: 1. Make the pipe safe. The seams must be secure so that individual joints cannot open up, and the various joints must be held securely together so that they can't accidentally separate. 2. Make the pipe uniform so that the sections don't have to be assembled in any special order. An exception is pipe that is intentionally tapered in order to nest one section inside the other.

Commercial stovepipe has a self-locking seam, crimping (to reduce one end enough to fit inside the uncrimped end of the next section) and a swedge (the swelling above the crimping that prevents one section from sliding too far into the next). Homemade pipe will have to include elements that duplicate or substitute for these features.

Perhaps the easiest way to make stovepipe is to roll each end of a sheet of flat stock around the crimped end of a joint of commercial stovepipe to form a uniform tube, both ends of which have the same diameter. Crimping can be added by twisting with a pair of needle-nose pliers, as shown in Figure 21.1, and a stop can be made by installing a sheet-metal screw about 2 inches from the uncrimped end. The seam can be secured either with pop rivets or sheet-metal screws.

A seam that requires no fasteners is shown in Figure 21.2. Two small flaps along the edges of the metal are mated and then pounded flat. The metal along one edge of the resulting four-ply seam is then flattened in such a way that the two halves can't pull apart again.

Many a stove in this part of Alaska is fitted with a simple damper made from a sheet of tin-can metal with a few folds at the end for a

173

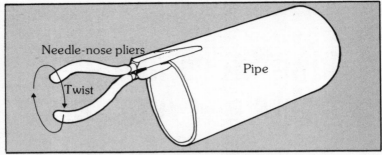

Figure 21.1 (*above*)—How to form crimping on homemade pipe.
Figure 21.2 (*below*)—A pipe seam that requires no fasteners. Designed by Oliver Cameron.

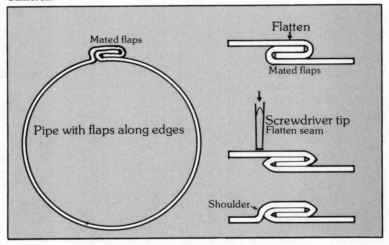

handle. The simplest kind is merely a flat sheet that slides in and out of a horizontal slit in the stovepipe (Figures 16.15 and 21.3, Drawing A). A somewhat more sophisticated type consists of a curved sheet riding in a slit that curves slightly downward (Figure 21.3, Drawing B). Instead of just sliding in and out, this type of damper also pivots about the end points of the slit.

With either style of damper, the inner end of the sheet is cut into a circular shape to match the curvature of the pipe. There should be some space for smoke to escape around the flat sides, so that the damper can be closed all the way without making the stove smoke. (That way, the stove can be shut down in one quick motion, without a lot of tiresome fine-tuning.) If the edge spaces don't

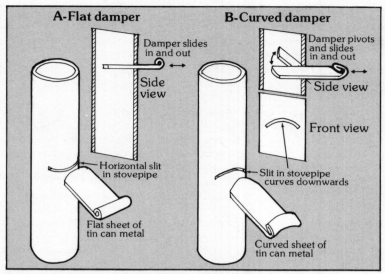

Figure 21.3—Flat and curved tin-can dampers. Designed by Keith Jones.

provide enough by-pass when the damper is fully closed, a hole of appropriate size can be cut into the middle of the sheet.

Ted Ledger has published a drawing of an entirely different sort of damper (Figure 21.4). Rather than controlling the fire by limiting the smoke flow from the stove, this sleeve damper spoils the draft by admitting air from the room into the pipe, much like the draft corrector described in Chapter 4.

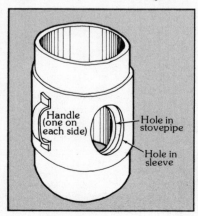

Figure 21.4—Ted Ledger's sleeve damper. The sleeve is rotated to expose or cover a hole in the stovepipe (from *Alternative Sources of Energy*, No. 14, May, 1974, p. 35).

175

A sleeve damper mounted just below a stovepipe oven would double as a secondary draft. When the stove is fired up for baking, the stack gases are bound to be hot enough for complete combustion to take place, but they may be somewhat deficient in oxygen. Secondary air entering the pipe just below the oven would encourage complete combustion of the smoke at the very point where the heat would do the most good.

You may go a long time without needing to make your own stovepipes or dampers, but chances are you will eventually run across a situation in which you'll need to make an adapter. We generally think of using adapters to connect one pipe to another of a different diameter, but, in practice, I've more often made adapters to satisfy my insistence that the crimped end of the stovepipe be placed *down* so that sooty condensate won't dribble out at every junction. In other words, I have often had to build a special adapter just to connect a 6-inch stovepipe to a 6-inch collar.

My neighbor recently encountered a situation that provides a good example. His range had a 7-inch stovepipe collar, sized for use with the crimped end up (the messy way), and his roof jack was sized for 6-inch pipe. Thus, he had two problems: first, to reduce the pipe from 7 to 6 inches, and second, to invert the whole thing so it wouldn't drip.

He bought a commercial adapter, and was able to put the stove into service. But since the adapter was also crimped the wrong way, so much condensate dribbled out of the joints in the pipe that a tarry deposit began to build up at the base of the pipe (Figure 21.5). It looked bad, smelled worse, and even caught fire a few times.

Figure 21.5—Build-up of creosote at the base of my neighbor's stovepipe, due to the use of an adapter with the crimped end up.

Next he pounded the crimps out of the adapter and inverted the pipe; now the pipe didn't streak, but all of the creosote leaked out where the adapter joined the stove. In his next attempt to solve the problem, he slit the adapter to try to make it fit *inside* the stovepipe collar, but that didn't work either.

Finally we made a proper adapter that fitted tightly inside the collar, preventing dripping, and that simultaneously reduced the

Figure 21.6—This homemade dripless adapter, fashioned by the author from a joint of 8-inch pipe, simultaneously inverts the stovepipe and reduces it from 7 to 6 inches.

pipe from 7 to 6 inches (Figure 21.6). This type of adapter is easy to make with only a few simple tools:

1. Obtain a piece of heavy-gauge commercial stovepipe, preferably galvanized, in a diameter 1 inch larger than the larger of the two elements to be connected.
2. Cut off the self-locking seam. The easiest way to do this without distorting the metal is to use a Bernz-cutter, available at most hardware stores (Figure 21.7). (Note: The little turned flap on the other edge of the pipe need not be removed, since it will be on the inside of the adapter.)

Figure 21.7—Removing the seam of a stovepipe with a Bernz-cutter. This tool does not distort the metal, as conventional tin snips do.

3. Form the uncrimped end of the adapter pipe around the crimped end of the next pipe up, squeeze it down tightly, and mark at the overlapping edge with a felt-tipped pen. Remove the adapter from the form, match up the mark, and clamp securely.

4. Form the crimped end into a circle and stick it into its receiver (either the stovepipe collar or the uncrimped end of the next pipe down, as the case may be). You will find it awkward to expand the pipe all the way so that the fit is snug, since it is hard to get a grip; but do the best you can and then mark the position (Figure 21.8). Remove the pipe, match up the mark again, and then allow the pipe to expand just enough to guarantee a snug fit. Clamp securely and drill a hole just above the crimping for the first rivet (or sheet-metal screw). Drive the rivet and unclamp the crimped end of the pipe.

5. Test the fit. If your estimate was correct, the fit will be just right, and you can go on to the next step. But don't feel bad if you have to remove the fastener, reestimate, clamp, drill, fasten and check again; usually it comes out right the second time. (The original hole will be blocked off, since the two sides of the seam will have shifted.)

6. Mark for the other rivets. Make the last mark 2 inches from the uncrimped end, to give clearance for the crimping on the adjoining pipe. The fasteners need not be spaced any closer than 3 inches.

7. Install a rivet next to the first one. Avoid the temptation to

178

Figure 21.8—Making the guide mark on the crimped end of the adapter. The pipe will be allowed to expand slightly to ensure a tight fit.

place the second rivet at the uncrimped end of the pipe to replace the clamp, because the finished adapter will not be lined up the same way it is at this stage. Remove the clamp at the uncrimped end of the pipe, realign the mark, and reclamp.

8. Install the third rivet next to the second one. *Now* you can do without the clamp at the far end of the pipe. Continue riveting *in the same direction* until all the rivets are in place. You'll notice that one edge of the seam protrudes farther at the end of the stovepipe than the other one does. This is because the adapter has a slightly conical shape. If you had started out by riveting both ends, the extra metal would now be distributed along the length of the pipe, and the seam would be puckered.

9. Finally, dress off the protruding edge at the uncrimped end of the adapter. Again, the Bernz-cutter is the handiest tool to use. Touch up the last rough edges with a file, and your dripless adapter is ready to install.

It is worth noting that makeshift adapters can also be fashioned from tin cans. A No. 10 can, for example, fits 6-inch stovepipe perfectly, and a hole can be cut in the closed end to receive 5- or 4-inch pipe. A 4-pound lard can makes a nice adapter for joining 6- and 5-inch pipes (Figure 21.9). And when I made the Three-Way Stove, I fashioned an elbow from an old spice can (Figure 13.17); the lid opening was just about right for 5-inch pipe, and I cut a hole in one side to admit the stovepipe collar. None of these adapters is really leakproof; but then, neither are most of the ones that are found on the shelves in the hardware store.

Figure 21.9—A lard-can adapter made by the author. Six-inch pipe fits into the open end of the can, and 5-inch pipe fits into the hole cut in the other end.

Chapter 22
Hot-Water Systems

A typical gas or electric hot-water heater ranks among the major energy users in the American household. If a wood stove supplies all or even part of the family's hot-water needs, the savings of energy can be significant.

The simplest hot-water system consists of a 5-gallon can and a kettle that sit on top of the stove. The can is for volume, the kettle for quick hot water. We find that this quantity of hot water—about 6 gallons—is enough to meet all of our household needs, except on

Figure 22.1—How to make a handle and a wooden lid for a five-gallon stove-top hot-water can.

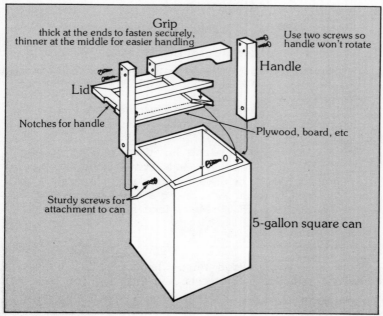

Grip
thick at the ends to fasten securely,
thinner at the middle for easier handling

Use two screws so
handle won't rotate

Handle

Lid

Notches for handle

Plywood, board, etc

Sturdy screws for
attachment to can

5-gallon square can

laundry day. Then we substitute a second 5-gallon can for the kettle and add a 16-gallon galvanized container as well.

Since a spill would be dangerous, I always attach sturdy handles to the 5-gallon cans. And since water in an open can steams up the room and doesn't get as hot as water in a closed container, I also use a simple wooden lid (Figure 22.1). To encourage heat absorption, I blacken the bottom of the can, and also the side that faces the stovepipe, with stove enamel (Figure 8.1).

How to Mend a Leaky Hot-Water Can

Rust eventually eats holes in the bottom of a hot-water can, especially if it is allowed to sit around empty, but wet. Most of the holes are very small, and are easily sealed with Weldwood Metal Mender, as follows:

1. Scour the rust off the inner and outer surfaces of the bottom of the can with steel wool. This will generally expose other pinholes that were still sealed with rust and hadn't leaked yet.
2. Locate the holes by looking against the light, and circle each one with a felt-tipped pen, both inside and outside the can.
3. Put a dab of Metal Mender on each hole from the *inside* of the can. The circles marking the holes enable you to work without having to hold the can up to the light.
4. Turn the can over and put another dab on each hole from the outside. The circles are very necessary on this side to locate the holes, which are now plugged from the inside and won't pass light.
5. Set the can in a warm place and allow the Metal Mender to dry overnight. (I always place mine on the stove top, upside down.)

These patches will withstand hot water indefinitely, and succeeding generations of holes can be treated in the same way. The can won't have to be discarded until a long hole opens up along the bottom seam. After losing a few cans this way, I learned to seal that seam with Metal Mender *before* putting a can into service.

Some commercial wood ranges feature built-in hot-water reservoirs, complete with faucets, and the same feature could certainly be built into a homemade stove. The tank should be of stainless steel or some other rust-resistant material, and provision should be made for cleaning the inevitable soot from any surface of the tank touched by the smoke.

More complex hot-water systems employ copper heating coils. In the system shown in Figure 22.2, cold water enters the firebox coil from the lower part of the tank, picks up heat, rises, and

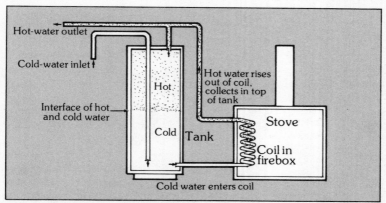

Figure 22.2—Firebox-coil hot-water system. The interface between hot and cold water gradually moves downward as water heats, and upward as hot water is drawn off and replaced by cold.

reenters the tank near the top. As the process continues, the interface between the hot and cold water slowly moves down the tank.

If the stove operates at a high setting for a long time and no hot water is drawn off, the interface eventually reaches the bottom of the tank, and hot water begins to enter the coil. Heat build-up is then rapid, and the water may actually boil. This sounds dangerous, but actually the pressure can't ever be greater than that of the incoming water main.

I had this sort of system in my bachelor days, when I lived in an old house in Anchorage. When the water in the tank got especially hot, I'd take the opportunity to throw a load of laundry into the washing machine. Talk about frugal! I'd even reclaim the heat by running the outlet from the washer into the bathtub and holding the wash water there until it went stone cold.

Since homes heated by wood stoves may have cold, damp walls at floor level where circulation is poor, it is appealing to think about a system whereby hot water from a coil in the firebox could be circulated through a baseboard heater of some sort. A small electric pump would make the project perfectly feasible, of course. But if there were no electricity, could the hot water be made to circulate by itself?

Since the inlet and outlet of such a system would both be at the same level, the hot water wouldn't be able to rise out of the coil, and so there wouldn't seem to be much chance of inducing self-circulation. But I know a man who claims to have gotten such a system to work by installing check valves in the line (Figure 22.3). When the water in the coil reaches the boiling point, it tends to boil

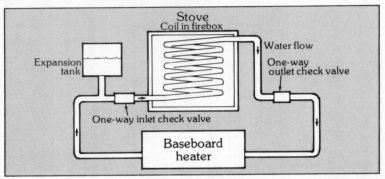

Figure 22.3 (*above*)—Self-circulating firebox-coil baseboard heater system. Modified from design by John Topkok.

Figure 22.4 (*left*)—Stovepipe hot-water unit sold in kit form by Blazing Showers Company. The unit is substituted for the first section of stovepipe.

Figure 22.5 (*right and overleaf*)—Greenbriar Hydronic system. Ready-made coils fit inside Greenbriar fireplaces, and the company also makes fittings for integrating the resulting hot-water output into various types of heating systems.

in surges. Each "bump" sends some hot water through the outlet check valve. During the brief interval of reduced pressure following each surge, water that has cooled after circulating around the system enters through the inlet check valve.

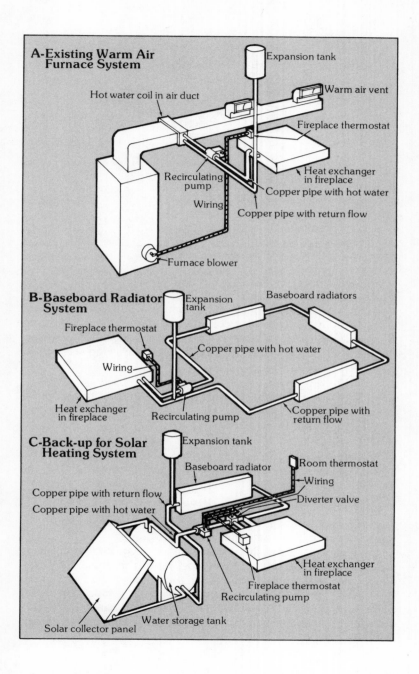

A-Existing Warm Air Furnace System

Expansion tank

Warm air vent

Hot water coil in air duct

Fireplace thermostat

Recirculating pump

Heat exchanger in fireplace

Wiring

Copper pipe with hot water

Copper pipe with return flow

Furnace blower

B-Baseboard Radiator System

Expansion tank

Baseboard radiators

Fireplace thermostat

Copper pipe with hot water

Wiring

Heat exchanger in fireplace

Recirculating pump

Copper pipe with return flow

C-Back-up for Solar Heating System

Expansion tank

Baseboard radiator

Room thermostat

Copper pipe with return flow

Wiring

Copper pipe with hot water

Diverter valve

Heat exchanger in fireplace

Fireplace thermostat

Recirculating pump

Solar collector panel

Water storage tank

185

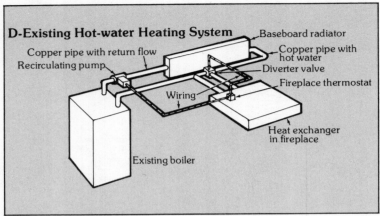

D-Existing Hot-water Heating System

Copper pipe with return flow
Recirculating pump
Baseboard radiator
Copper pipe with hot water
Diverter valve
Fireplace thermostat
Wiring
Heat exchanger in fireplace
Existing boiler

Figure 22.5 (*continued*) — Greenbriar Hydronic system.

Hot-water coils are usually placed in the firebox, but suitable results can also be obtained from coils placed in or around the stovepipe, or in the chimney. A company called Blazing Showers offers ready-made stovepipe coils that can be attached to a wood stove and connected to a hot-water tank (Figure 22.4). Greenbriar Products sells ready-made coils that fit inside their fireplaces, along

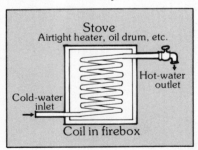

Stove
Airtight heater, oil drum, etc.
Hot-water outlet
Cold-water inlet
Coil in firebox

Figure 22.6 — Chip-heater hot-water system.

with fittings for integrating the resulting hot-water output into various types of heating systems (Figure 22.5).

In Australia we ran into yet another type of copper-coil hot-water system — the chip heater. Most homes in Australia's rural areas have at least one wood-stave water tank tucked under the eaves. A chip heater fits in very nicely with this ecologically sound water supply, since it operates only when hot water is actually needed and fires up quite nicely on chips of wood, pieces of bark and other scraps, including trash.

186

Figure 22.7—Oil-drum dog-food cooker. The same system can be used to heat laundry water in quantity. Collection of Pete MacManus.

The body of a chip heater (Figure 22.6) is similar to a standard airtight heater, from which one could easily be made. Water is piped through the firebox coil to the point of use, where the faucet is located. The temperature of the emerging water is determined both by the intensity of the fire and by the rate at which water is allowed to flow out of (not *into*) the coil—the smaller the trickle, the hotter the water. Our particular chip heater was out in the washing shed, next to the bathtub, so the fire also took the chill off the room. It was even possible to add more fuel to the heater without getting out of the soak.

Figure 22.7 shows one more possibility for heating water in quantity. This unit happens to be a dog-food cooker, but the same sort of system can be used for heating water. The tank is made from the lower third of a barrel, and the firebox is just a section of the middle of the same drum, with a stokehole and a smoke outlet cut into it. The remaining third of the barrel would provide plenty of metal for fashioning a proper door, draft system, and stovepipe collar, if desired.

Chapter 23
Epilogue

Ken Kern, in his article "Heating and Cooking with Wood," offered the opinion that "in recent years, more wood heaters have been put together in small blacksmith and backyard welding shops than in all stove foundries combined." It would be hard to gather statistics on something like this, but two things are certain: (1) a lot of people are making a lot of interesting stoves; and (2) for the most part, they are working independently, largely unaware of the work of others and unable to profit from it.

Alternative-energy enthusiasts who are working with wind power or solar heating have their own journals, and are exchanging stimulating accounts of individual work and experimentation in their rapidly evolving fields. But as far as I know, there has never been any significant nationwide exchange of information among and between stove builders. Wood-stove information is scattered in bits and pieces among a variety of publications that somehow touch upon the simple life.

This is bound to change. When the *Whole Earth Catalog* burst upon the scene some years ago, it tapped a previously undiscovered lode of interest that surprised even the editors. I have a hunch that the interest in homemade wood stoves also runs deeper than anybody has previously suspected, and that stove builders will eventually have their own organization and periodical. There already exists a more general periodical on wood stoves and alternative sources of energy (see Bibliography).

In the meantime, this seems to be the only book ever published on designing and making wood stoves. If you are aware of an idea or a design that doesn't appear in these pages, I'd be grateful if you'd send it along, so that it can be added to the growing body of information to be shared with all those who seek to extend their proficiency in the art.

Appendix:
List of Manufacturers

For the benefit of those who would rather buy than build, I have pulled together the following list of manufacturers of wood stoves and related equipment. Readers may scan the list to find manufacturers that offer the kinds of units that are under consideration, and then write for brochures. (I would like to suggest sending a stamped, self-addressed envelope with each request, in order to ease the burden of postal and labor costs on the companies.)

The letters printed after each of the addresses refer to the types of units available from that particular company, and are keyed to the descriptions in Chapter 2, as follows:

A	. . . . . Airtight heater	GR	. . . . Galley range
BSI	. . . . Box stove (cast iron)	HE	. . . . Heat Exchanger
BSK	. . . Barrel stove kit	K	. . . . . Kitchen heater
BSS	. . . Box stove (sheet steel)	LH	. . . . Laundry heater
C	. . . . . Cabinet heater	MF	. . . . Marine fireplace
CaS	. . . Caboose stove	PB	. . . . Pot-bellied stove
CH	. . . . Cabin heater	PS	. . . . Parlor stove
CoS	. . . Collapsible stove	SH	. . . . Standing heater
CR	. . . . Combination range	WC	. . . Wood cookstove
DH	. . . . Drum heater	WF	. . . . Wood furnace
DS	. . . . Downdraft stove	WR	. . . . Wood range
F	. . . . . . Franklin stove	WWH	. Wood-fired water
FF	. . . . . Freestanding fireplace-		heater
	stove		

Ashley Automatic Heater
  Company (C, A)
  Box 730
  Sheffield, Alabama 35660

Atlanta Stove Works, Inc.
  (WR, C, A, F, PB, PS, LH,
  BSI, WC)
  Box 5254
  Atlanta, Georgia 30307

Autocrat Corp. (C)
New Athens, Illinois 62264

Bellway Manufacturing (WF)
Grafton, Vermont 05146

Birmingham Stove and Range
Company (A, BSI, C, F,
LH, PB, PS, WC, WR)
1700 Vanderbilt Road
Birmingham, Alabama
35234

Blazing Showers (WWH)
Box 327
Point Arena, California
95468

Brown Stove Works, Inc. (C)
Box 490
Cleveland, Tennessee
37311

Calcinator Corp. (BSS)
28th and Water Streets
Bay City, Michigan
48706

Colorado Tent & Awning
Company (BSS),
3333 East 52nd Avenue
Denver, Colorado 80216

Cowanesque Valley Iron
Works, Inc. (PB, CaS)
964 Elm Street
Cowanesque, Pennsylvania
16918

Cyclops Corp.
Empire-Detroit
Steel Division (A)
Dover, Ohio 44622

Dynapac, Inc. (CoS)
1610 Industrial Road
Salt Lake City, Utah 84104

Fatsco (CH, BSK)
251 North Fair Avenue
Benton Harbor, Michigan
49022

Fire-View Distributors (FF)
Box 370
Rogue River, Oregon
97537

Fisher Stove Works (BSS)
135 Commercial
Springfield, Oregon 97477

Fisher's Products (BSK,
glass-door style)
Route 1, Box 63
Conifer, Colorado 80433

Garden Way Research (BSS)
Charlotte, Vermont 05445

Greenbriar Products Inc.
(FF, WWH)
Box 473
Spring Green, Wisconsin
53588

HS Kedler
(See Tekton Design Corp.)

Jackes-Evans Manufacturing
Company (A)
4427 Geraldine Avenue
St. Louis, Missouri 63115

Jøtul
(see Kristia Associates)

190

Kickapoo Stove Works, Ltd.
(BSS)
Main Street
La Farge, Wisconsin 54639

King Products Division, Martin
Industries (WR, C, A, F,
PB, PS, LH, BSS, WC)
Box 128
Florence, Alabama 35630

KNT, Inc. (FF)
Box 25
Hayesville, Ohio 44838

Kristia Associates (FF, SH,
BSI)
Box 1118
Portland, Maine 04104
(U.S. distributor of Jøtul
stoves from Norway)

Lange
(see Scandinavian Stoves,
Inc.)

Larry Gay Stove Works, Inc.
(BSS)
Marlboro, Vermont 05344

Locke Stove Company
(C, DH)
114 West 11th Street
Kansas City, Missouri
64105

Longwood Furnace Corp.
(WF)
Gallatin, Missouri 64640

Louisville Tin & Stove
Company (A)
Box 1079
Louisville, Kentucky 40201

Malleable Iron Range
Company (WR, K, C, F,
FF, CR)
Beaver Dam, Wisconsin
53916

Malm Fireplaces, Inc. (F)
368 Yolanda Avenue
Santa Rosa, California
95404

Marathon Heater Company,
Inc. (WF)
Route 2, Box 165
Marathon, New York
13803

Marcade Winnwood (BSK)
1833 Chicadee Drive
Knoxville, Tennessee
37919
(also see Modern Kit Sales)

Merry Music Box (WR, SH)
10 McKown Street
Boothbay Harbor, Maine
04538
(U.S. distributor of
Styria stoves from Austria)

Modern Kit Sales (FF, BSS,
BSK, WWH)
Box 12501
North Kansas City, Missouri
64116

Modern Machine and Welding
(WF)
2307 Highway 2 West
Grand Rapids, Minnesota
55744

Monogram Industries, Inc. (C)
Quincy, Illinois 62301

Morsø
(see Southport Stoves
Division)

Old Stove Company (WR, PB,
BSI, WC)
Box 7617
Dallas, Texas 75209

Patented Manufacturing
Company (HE)
Bedford Road
Lincoln, Massachusetts
01773

Portland Stove Foundry,
Inc.(WR, K, F, FF,
PB, PS, BSI)
57 Kennebec Street
Portland, Maine 04104

Richmond Ring Company
Shipmate Stove Division
(GR, CH, MF)
Souderton, Pennsylvania
18964

Riteway Manufacturing
Company (C, WF)
Box 6
Harrisonburg, Virginia
22801

Sam Daniels Company (WF)
Box 868
Montpelier, Vermont
05602

Scandinavian Stoves, Inc.
(BSI, PS)
Box 72
Alstead, New Hampshire
03602
(U.S. distributor of
Lange stoves from
Denmark)

Shenandoah Manufacturing
Company, Inc. (A, BSS)
Box 839
Harrisonburg, Virginia
22801

Skaggs Manufacturing and
Foundry Company (WF)
Box 157
Crocker, Missouri 65452

Southport Stoves (FF, BSI)
248 Tolland Street
East Hartford, Connecticut
06108
(U.S. distributor for
Morsø stoves from
Denmark)

Tekton Design Corp. (WF)
Conway, Massachusetts
01341
(U.S. distributor of HS
Kedler furnaces from
Denmark)

Torrid Mfg. Co. Inc. (BSS, HE)
1248 Poplar Place South
Seattle, Washington 98144

Union Manufacturing
Company, Inc.
(BSI, LH, PB)
Sixth and Washington
Streets
Boyertown, Pennsylvania
19512

Union Stove Works, Inc. (CaS)
12 Columbia Avenue
Paterson, New Jersey
07503

United States Stove Company
(C, F, BSS)
Box 151
South Pittsburg, Tennessee
37380

Vermont Woodstove
Company (DS)
307 Elm Street
Bennington, Vermont
05201

Washington Stove Works
(WR, K, C, A, F, FF, PB,
PS, GR, CoS, CH, BSI,
BSK)
Box 687
Everett, Washington 98206

Whitten Enterprises, Inc. (BSS)
Box 798
Bennington, Vermont
05201

Will-Burt Company (C)
202 South Main Street
Orrville, Ohio 44667

Winnwood
(see Modern Kit Sales)

Bibliography

Buyer's Guide to Woodstoves. Bennington, VT: Vermont Wood Stove Co., 1975.

Coleman, Peter. *Wood Stove Know-how.* Charlotte, VT: Garden Way, 1974.

Gay, Larry. *The Complete Book of Heating with Wood.* Charlotte, VT: Garden Way, 1974.

Kern, Ken. "Heating and Cooking with Wood." In *Producing Your Own Power,* edited by C. H. Stoner. Emmaus, PA: Rodale, 1974.

Ledger, Ted. "Build Your Own Wood Stove." *Alternative Sources of Energy,* no. 14 (May 1974), pp. 35-36.

Rombauer, Irma S., and Becker, Marion R. *Joy of Cooking.* Indianapolis: Bobbs-Merrill, 1964.

Ross, Bob, and Ross, C. *Modern and Classic Woodburning Stoves and the Grass Roots Energy Revival.* Woodstock, NY: The Overlook Press, 1977.

Shelton, Jay. *Woodburner's Encyclopedia.* Williamstown, MA: Jay Shelton.

Sundance and Louie. *Blazing Showers: Stovepipe Water Heater Manual.* Point Arena, CA: Blazing Showers, 1975.

Vivian, John. *Wood Heat.* Emmaus, PA: Rodale, 1976.

Wik, Ole. *How to Build an Oil Barrel Stove.* Anchorage: Alaska Northwest, 1976.

Periodical

Woodburning Quarterly and Home Energy Digest, 8009 34th Street South, Minneapolis, MN 55420.